Avoid 1-Click Shopping if You Have Parkinson's

...and other tips for dealing with Parkinson's Disease

Michael Beetner

Published 2013 by Shaky Ventures of the Carolinas

152 Old Post Rd., Mooresville, NC 28117

ISBN: 09776011331X

ISBN-13: 978-0-9760113-1-6

To Sandy

Foreword

When I was a lad growing up in the 1940s, I would always listen to Walter Winchell give the news on Sunday night radio. He always began by saying, "Good evening Mr. and Mrs. America and all the ships at sea. Let's go to press." I was thrilled to hear him say that.

I thought of becoming a radio announcer when I grew up, but I soon realized that everyone referred to Walter Winchell as the "columnist" rather than the "radio announcer." I decided at an early age to become a columnist first and the radio program would surely follow.

In grade school, I subscribed to *My Weekly Reader,* but I was disappointed by the lack of a columnist.

Years later, after maturing to a more advanced grade, I joined the junior high school journalism class, which published the *Oak Street Gazette.* Some of you may not have heard of it. It's just as well. I was appointed staff photographer because I had a camera. I never had a chance to write a thing.

I tried again in high school by joining the school paper but, I was assigned to the sports page because there were only three boys in the class and I was needed there. I had no interest in sports so the other two boys got to handle all of the big games and I was relegated to intramural events between homerooms. This assignment did not involve lengthy descriptions of the games, but rather an accurate tally of results and standings. My only challenge was to select the verb that most accurately described the score, e.g. "Room 201

Trounces Room 104 by 86-58," or "Room 110 Edges Room 112 by Single Point."

Since there seemed no demand for male columnists, I went on to other studies. Walter Winchell passed on and was not replaced.

Later in life, when I reached what is euphemistically called "the golden years," I learned I had a thing called Parkinson's. Disease (PD) As I became more involved in Parkinson's, I was elected president of the Central Ohio Parkinson's Society (COPS). COPS had a monthly newsletter and my predecessor had begun a monthly President's Column. I took this to be a sign of apology from God for the inconvenience that Parkinson's was causing me. At last I had my opportunity to write a column and something to write about.

This book is an edited selection of those columns. My intent was to write about the various aspects of Parkinson's from the patient's perspective. I assume their narrow interest is what has kept me from getting a radio program.

Some of these columns have appeared before in a book titled *Smile if You Have Parkinson's*. The book briefly made it to the bottom of the listing of the *New York Times* top 32,000 best selling books. Collectors now search for the rare, non-autographed copies. Beyond that, almost all of them appeared in the COPS Newsletter. However, they can be considered only slightly used.

Contents

Introduction

I read where the Reverend Billy Graham once described his Parkinson's as "a blessing." My first thought was that he must have a different form of Parkinson's than I. Then, there is the obvious—he has a greater faith than I.

The same article referred to Dr. Graham as "the Reverend Billy Graham, who is afflicted with Parkinson's Disease..." What a great term— "afflicted." I can identify with that. Like over a million other Americans, I awake each morning and begin a daily struggle with my own body. Slowly, without a single holiday from symptoms, Parkinson's works at depriving me of control of my own body. My limbs do not move as quickly and fluidly as before. I do not naturally swing my arms when I walk. Muscles that do not move much, atrophy and we become stiff and tight especially in the neck and shoulders. Our voices become faint and our face no longer records our expressions. We do not smile as we used to.

I think this crosses the line. I was born and raised in Iowa some seventy-odd years ago, where displays of emotion were discouraged (If you thought I was going to write, "frowned upon," you are from Iowa as well.) In Iowa in those days, the only public display of emotion permitted was humor, and then only if in an ironic or self-deprecating form.

This was required by society for its self-preservation. What with the price of corn and hogs, to say nothing of the weather, if gloom and misery could be freely expressed in

Iowa, little else could get done. Parkinson's patients can learn from this.

Iowans always smile as they greet other Iowans and also flash a smile whenever a small courtesy is extended them, such as selling them a newspaper. The smile may be quick and fleeting, but always just long enough to be seen by the other person, who can check it off their list and feel comfortable. This is where Parkinson's patients, even those from Iowa, often fail. A smile no longer comes naturally and effortlessly to our lips. We must force it out. If we do not force it out, we risk sending an incorrect societal message. People do not like to deal with people they feel are hostile or unfriendly.

You say Parkinsonians have less to be happy about than Iowans? Friend, you have not looked at the prices being paid for corn and hogs lately. Iowans long ago decided in concert that they may as well laugh at it because crying is no more effective and less satisfying. If we can't laugh at Parkinson's, what can we laugh at? (A true Iowan would say *anyone* could laugh at a Minnesotan.)

This wisdom did not come to me simply because of my birthplace. To be honest, when I was first diagnosed with Parkinson's ("PD" as we shall call it from this point on) it did not seem particularly funny to me at the time. I busied myself learning all I could about my affliction. This led me to the Central Ohio Parkinson's Society (hereafter referred to as "COPS"). I attended my first support group meeting and, later, became president of COPS.

COPS is a charity that provides services and information about PD at no charge. It also publishes a large, monthly newsletter. I had wanted to be a writer all of my life but, rather than starve my family as I wrote the great American novel, I followed a career in computers.

In my new role as president, I began by writing the president's column about the state of the society and all of the traditional items that were of no interest outside the board room. I quickly bored even myself of that, so I began to write about the various issues involved in living with PD. A creative writing instructor once told me to write from my experience background. For me, that was Iowa. The reaction to the first couple of columns was very positive—at least from family members and other Iowans on the mailing list of about 3,000. It turns out that people like to smile even with PD.

This book is a compilation of some of those columns. They have been scrubbed a little and brought up to date where necessary.

As the non-writing workload at COPS increased, I realized that I was attending too many funerals and too few weddings so I retired again, this time to write. Someone later explained to me the funeral/wedding problem was that funerals do not require an invitation.

But, now, I am doing something I like. This is my blessing from PD.

My Short Career as a Labor Leader

Having been elected as your new president, the vetting process makes it necessary that I provide background data about my past leadership positions.

I grew up in Burlington, Iowa, in a family of very modest means. We did own our own home, purchased in 1945 and secured with a $2,000 mortgage to be paid over 30 years. My father worked for the J.I. Case Company, at that time making combines at the Burlington plant. Workers there were ill-treated, as was common for the period. Dad was one of the leaders in forming the union. The union was a local of the United Auto Workers.

Over many years and a strike or two, Case workers negotiated better wages, medical coverage, paid vacations, paid holidays, and pensions. There were a number of strong unions in town at the time and Burlington was known as a "union" town.

So when Eagle Super Markets, a grocery business located in Moline, Illinois, decided to build their first store outside of the Quad Cities in Burlington, they took careful note of the unions. This was in 1954 before there were franchises of all types. Then, all grocery was local. In fact, the concept of a supermarket was new to a town where grocery stores were small and scattered about in neighborhoods. There was much for people to accept and adjust to in this new age of grocery buying. For the first time Burlingtonians saw meat packaged pre-cut in little plastic trays. For people who had gone to butcher shops all of their lives and approved of the cut before it was wrapped in brown paper, this was a sea-change. It was not the meat that attracted shoppers, but rather the better prices and greater selection.

The Eagle people wanted this first out-of-town experiment to work, so they pulled out all of the stops, including arriving with a union already in place to satisfy the "this is a union town mentality." They also paid sixty cents an hour (with time-and-a-half on Sundays) for part-time workers, big money for the times. You had to be 16 years old to work there and in May of 1955 I was only 14. I solved this problem by exaggerating my year of birth.

We were very hard workers and the store began to rely on us part-timers more and more. Many of us worked more than forty hours a week and had ordering and stocking responsibilities for different sections of the store.

The union was The Retail Clerks of America, Local 1470. We had never heard of them before and the whole union thing was new to us. The union people were in the Quad Cities and only appeared for monthly meetings to collect dues. They referred to each other using the title of "brother" or "sister." Sister Fleece was the secretary and dues collector. She attended every meeting to collect dues and another gentleman (whose name escapes me) was the organizer.

We elected a president from among those full-timers and very little ever happened, perhaps as the owners wanted. In 1957 there was our annual meeting to elect the president. The union's candidate that year was an old fellow who had little ambition and was one of the slowest people on the planet. Looking around the room, there were only four full-time people present and none really wanted the job.

I volunteered. Sister Fleece tried to squash that by pointing out I was part-time. I asked which part of the constitution forbade part-timers from the presidency. She allowed as how there was no such language there, but that "it just made good sense" that the president be full-time.

So, with no specific language to the contrary, I was elected. The duties of the office were vague. Sister Fleece handled all of the funds and there were no issues with management leaving me free to continue work and attend high school.

Several months later, our organizer attended the monthly meeting with word that the Retail Clerks were on strike against Montgomery-Ward and it was not going well. While Burlington did have a Montgomery-Ward store, we were the only Retail Clerks in town.

I was eager to demonstrate that I could be a man of action in my new role, so I volunteered to distribute a flyer written by the union's national people about the issues and what bad people the management of Wards were and how the chain should be boycotted. The next morning found me and a couple of recruits at the main gate of J. I. Case, handing out flyers to arriving workers. The flyers were all passed out in plenty of time to get me to the start of my high school day feeling good about my assistance to my remote brothers and sisters.

About 10 a.m. our principal, Mr. Pease, appeared in our classroom and asked me to step out into the hall. There he told me that I had an urgent phone call down in the office. Schools in those days did not take calls for students. My first thought was that my family had somehow been killed in a calamity, which could be the only situation that would warrant Mr. Pease interrupting my education and his schedule. Seeing the panic on my face, he said it was a Mr. Domonic Salvetore and he was insisting on speaking with me at once.

I had never heard the name before, so I asked if he was sure it was me that he wanted. "Oh yeah," Mr. Pease allowed.

When we arrived at the main office, Mr. Pease said I could use his office and phone and I should just pick up line one. I was sure this had never happened in the history of Burlington High School.

Trying to keep my voice from squeaking, I said "Hello."

"Are you the kid who was passing out flyers at Case this morning?" the voice asked. I replied in the affirmative.

"Why in the hell are you doing that?"

I explained that the Retail Clerks were on strike against Montgomery-Ward and that I was helping my union brothers with their struggle.

"The local people here are not on strike."

I acknowledged, that saying not all Ward's stores were organized.

"But the Burlington store is organized and is not on strike and you should not be advocating a boycott against them."

Here, I figured the guy is really off track.

"The Burlington store is not organized" I said, further explaining "I'm sure of that because I am president of the local and there are no Wards employees there."

"Well, I'm the business manager of the Teamsters and they are organized under our union," he shouted, his rising anger showing.

"The Ward's clerks are teamsters?" I asked incredulously.

"Have been for years."

"Really?" I was dumbfounded.

"You *do* recognize these people as fellow unionists, don't you?"

I thought for a moment.

"Teamsters are truck drivers. Those clerks are not truck drivers. We don't recognize that." I was setting some new policy here, I could tell.

Now he began to threaten. "If you don't stop this crap, you are going to be in a heap of trouble."

I couldn't think of anything else to say, so I said, "Goodbye."

"Is everything OK?" asked Mr. Pease on my way out.

"Yep," I assured him.

About an hour later I was in a different class when Mr. Pease appeared at the door again. "You have another call."

This one was from Harry Taylor, the Store Manager of the local Eagles. I wondered what he had said to cause Mr. Pease to repeat the history-shattering handling of telephone calls to students.

Harry was genuinely confused. "I don't know what is going on," he began, "but Dick Waxman just called and told me to fire you at once. He said that something you had done had caused the teamsters to stop work moving our trucks and that they would be leading a boycott of our stores."

Dick Waxman was president of the entire Eagle Food Center chain. He was not in the habit of speaking with store managers directly and Harry could have received a call from God himself with less of a surprise.

"What did you do?" Harry asked.

I explained and he said it was too bad but that I was not to come in to work after school, my having been fired and all. Calling up all of my gumption, I told Harry that he cannot fire an employee for union activities on the job, let alone off the job.

Harry said "If Dick Waxman says you're fired, you're fired."

I decided to call the district organizer that had provided the flyers and find out for certain my rights. I asked Mr. Pease if I could make a long distance call on this phone. He decided that enough history had been made that day and that perhaps I should go home and use my own phone. He also felt that I should handle any phone calls that were emergencies at home before returning to school.

After numerous phone calls with me or on my behalf, a compromise was reached. I would stop passing out leaflets and the Teamsters would go back to work and I would get my job back. The compromise worked, but the bad blood between the Teamsters and me endured.

Allow me to give you a little more background before I continue. Burlington had a building known as "The Labor Temple" where many different unions had offices. This was after the AFL and CIO had merged—the golden years of the labor movement. To promote labor harmony, all of the union locals sent a representative to a monthly meeting called the Trades and Labor Assembly. I was the Retail Clerk's representative.

During this period, scandal broke out in the Teamsters International. Jimmie Hoffa and, then-president Dave Beck were cited by the government for corruption. They were then thrown out of the AFL–CIO. This delighted me because I expected that at the next Trades and Labor meeting I could witness their expulsion from our group. Sweet justice.

At the next meeting, I waited for the subject to come up. When the motion to adjourn was made after all of the old and new business was dispatched, I jumped to my feet to object. I re-stated the obvious about what the Teamsters had done and our obligation through the AFL–CIO to throw the bums out. All hell broke loose. The Teamsters objected to my objection and the meeting was quickly adjourned.

The next day the Teamster Business Manager suggested that I stop by his office there at the Labor Temple so that we might avoid a repeat of past unpleasantness. His office was dimly lit and he wore a leather jacket, making the whole scene rather intimidating.

He began by telling me that his local had done nothing wrong and that the Trades and Labor Assembly would never throw them out. I replied that they had no choice but to throw them out, given what had happened on the national level. Dominick was not used to a snot–nosed, high school kids telling him things he didn't want to hear.

"Do you know why they will never throw us out?" he asked again, struggling with his rising anger. "Because we own this Labor Temple building."

"I think people will do the right thing," I replied.

Did I intend to bring it up again at the next meeting, he wanted to know? "Of course," I replied. At this point he was kind enough to share with me his concern for my personal safety if this reckless behavior persisted.

True to my word, I brought the motion to expel the Teamsters from the Trades and Labor Assembly. There were only two votes to expel–mine and my father's. Years later they were finally expelled.

I continued as president (although with a lower profile) until the spring of 1959. It was time to renegotiate our contract and I was going to be the central figure at the bargaining table. My constituency was the part-timers, many of whom worked more than forty hours per week in the summer and other times but, being part-time, did not receive paid holidays and vacations. I set about to correct this egregious error. I proposed that part-timers receive prorated vacations and holidays as well as a substantial pay raise.

I realized this was going to be a tough sell, so first I got the support of the part-timers at the store. This was easy. Next, I used the skills learned from the high school debate team to prepare a presentation and the debate points to back it up. I practiced over and over because this was to be my moment.

The first negotiating meeting was held in a hotel in Davenport. I wanted to be fresh and alert, so I had to leave the Spring Festival at Burlington Junior College early so that I might get a good night's rest. Those that followed the keg of beer to a small cemetery to avoid the police did not succeed. Many of my classmates were arrested.

The first negotiating session was a big disappointment. The Eagle executives arrived very late, complaining that they were missing dinner. Before we could present our demands, they told of bad business conditions and their losses. They said they wanted to cut pay in this new contract, but, in the interest of putting the whole thing behind them, they would agree to extend the present contract. We could take it or leave it, but they were leaving. And then they did leave.

The National Clerks sent a man who was a professional negotiator in to help. After the abrupt session, the national man asked what I was going to suggest for the new contract. I gave him my pitch and he thought I was insane. Never had part-time employees enjoyed such benefits. Eagles would never agree. I didn't have a backup plan, so I was committed to my original proposal.

It took a month and a strike vote to get them to the bargaining table again. This time I did get to present our demands. They listened, laughing at times, and summed things up with a simple "Never" before again walking out. This walking out was irritating because we were paying for the hotel room used for negotiations.

Finally, a few days before the deadline, we met and they accepted the part-time benefit principle. The fellow from the National office almost fell off his chair. So now we were down to negotiating only the fine points. First, the Eagle people explained the extreme hardship this would place on their accounting if all part-timers were covered. Take a person working three hours a week. Was that person to be given a 3/40th of a holiday? I could understand that. I suggested 20 hours should be the minimum because this would mean an easy half-pay for holidays. They wanted a thirty-hour minimum. We settled on 24. This still would not exclude anybody I knew. In the end, we settled for an additional fifteen cents an hour wage increase as well. I had gotten my dream contract.

Back in Burlington, I was received as a hero. That feeling continued up until the work schedules were posted for the upcoming week. Harry explained a new policy that part-timers would not be permitted to work more than twenty hours a week from then on—with no exceptions. I had been had. I decided to give up the unionism and go away to college.

Terrorism in Iowa, circa 1958

For certain, Rock 'n Roll was invented while I was in high school and, upon reflection, perhaps terrorism had its roots in Iowa at that time. I remember a newspaper story at the time began, "In an attempt to terrorize a group of girl scouts..." I have, dear reader, inside information on this case.

It seems that during their formative high-school years, a couple of my friends set off small explosive devices (fire crackers) near the sleeping quarters (tents) of a local paramilitary group (Girl Scouts) with the intent of scaring or, as the sheriff said later in the press, to "terrorize" them.

Two of the perpetrators were friends of mine. One was named (for the purposes of this article) Steve Stenstrom. Steve came from a good home and was thought by many to be a typical God-fearing, upstanding Iowa youth. Who knew?

His mother, whom we will call Clara Stenstrom(although that is her real name), took the news pretty hard. You can imagine how she must have felt once the press had splashed their name around. Actually, I don't think we can understand what that woman felt. She had obviously failed as a mother, but she resolved to make amends. She began, as she felt she must, by resigning her position as Sunday School teacher, explaining that not only was there the disgrace, but she felt she could no longer be the role model for children the position required and that her new duties of rehabilitating her wayward son would be taking additional time.

The case was solved due to some outstanding investigatory work by the county sheriff's officers. It came out during the interviews with the Girl Scouts that several of the girls had seen the boys laughing and knew their names. Back at headquarters, the officers employed the phone book to look up the boys' addresses and they were quickly apprehended.

Through all of this mess, I remained friends with Steve and we are friends to this day. He lives in Summit, N.J., using the same name. He even married and raised two fine daughters who, I am sure, know nothing of his sordid past.

Friends are an important part of your life, especially if you have PD. Friends accept you for who you are and who you have been, tremor or no. Visiting friends is a reason to get out of the house and enjoy some of the simple, but best, treasures of life. The biggest error one can make as a Parkie is to shun human contact and become a recluse. Yet many do just that because they are embarrassed by their shaking, drooling, soft voice or other indignities PD inflicts upon us. But, that is why God invented friends and made them totally accepting.

You must do your part. Keep in contact with your old friends who are distant from you. Write letters, e-mails, or notes if you can, or use the telephone. Most of us old fellows still have in the back of our minds that long distance telephone is expensive. It's dirt cheap anymore. More likely than not, it is free. Resolve today to call or email an old friend and catch up. Remember with him the days of your youth and the fun you had. The statute of limitations has passed for much of that now.

If you find yourself short of old friends, replacements can be found at your local PD support group meeting. You already have something in common.

If Steve could overcome his youth, you can overcome PD.

Life's Little Indignities

All indications are that there is a formal conspiracy afoot to steadily increase the difficulties we PD patients experience daily. How else can one explain the use of packaging for food and other products that is all but impossible to open? I can't tell you how many times I have to struggle and struggle to open even the lowliest of products.

Recently on a trip, U.S. Air presented me with a half-ounce package of "Trail Mix." I took this as a thank you for my flying 1800 miles with them and their way to apologize for my having to hold my knees to my chest or risk their being crushed by the seat in front of me, as well as for the numerous delays that pushed my arrival from 8:31 p.m. to 2:00 a.m.

Why would a small package of "food" be next to impossible to open? Now that I look back, I'm not sure it was food. Perhaps it was simply ballast in what was meant to be a survivor's souvenir.

It could also be that the FDA insisted that the contents either have clearly labeled ingredients (3 mini pretzels, various broken bits of stale breakfast cereal, various twigs and pebbles) or that the package be made impenetrable. Other governmental regulations classify any device brought on board to help open packages as a deadly weapon that cannot be allowed in the passenger compartment.

But the real outrage happened just last week. I want to share with you what may be the crown jewel of indignities. For seventy years now I have worn underwear. For seventy years I have put them on just as my mother taught me–label to the back. For seventy years my underwear has given me no trouble.

Last week I put on a new pair of boxer shorts my wife had purchased. They, at first, didn't feel comfortable but I thought it was because they were new. Regular readers will recall that I suffer from what the doctors call "urgency," which means my bladder is either quiescent or screaming for relief. Answering nature's call in a public restroom, I could not find the opening in the front of my new shorts. My manual dexterity is declining and it not unusual for me to have a bit of trouble, but I never had this much trouble.

After probably three minutes of pawing my private area with increasing desperation (and arousing the disgust of the other men there), I repaired to a stall to discover that the manufacturer had placed the label in the front. I later checked the others from the package and they were all like that. What could the manufacturer been thinking other than, "Let's have a little fun with those with Parkinson's?" I'm sure my dance was better than they had hoped for.

I cannot tell you exactly who in our government is behind this conspiracy. I suspect Senator Orin Hatch is the committee chair, judging from his highly buttoned-up appearance. Strom Thurman was probably a member, since his inability to recognize where he is would ensure his secrecy.

What can one do to fight back? I'd like to say that we should boycott manufacturers that use impenetrable packaging, but we would probably starve to death. I've written David Letterman, suggesting that he invite CEO's of some of the worst offenders to his show and ask them to open their product on live TV.

You can ask your pharmacist to package your drugs in old-fashioned, non-locking containers if there is no danger of young children having access to them.

Other than that, you can take my approach of cursing those responsible (optional) and then laughing at the absurdity of it all (required). Attitude is as important as medicine in PD. You're too old to cry about your PD. You never see Orin Hatch laughing. I see those struggling with PD laughing all of the time. This means we are winning. God is just and, I'm sure, there is a special corner in hell for packaging designers.

Chin Up Iowans

The other day I met a gentleman who knew my wife through business. He recognized the last name and asked me, "Are you Sandy Beetner's father?"

I have not found a witty reply yet to this question, apparently based on my looking twenty years older than I am, and/or my wife looking twenty years younger than she is. This has happened before, often when traveling by air with my daughters. Wheel chair attendants will invariably try to strike up a conversation by asking one of the girls where they are traveling to with their "grandfather." Now that I think about it, this pretty much shoots down the "young looking wife" hypothesis.

Whenever I get depressed about my advancing age, I think of my grandmother in Iowa. I never saw her depressed once in her life. To her, "life was life" and you played the hand you were dealt. Grandpa had PD. Back then, when your PD appeared, the doctor would tell you that you had "shaking palsy" and there was nothing that could be done. How many sleepless nights did they endure because of Grandpa's tremors? I can't imagine a world without Sinemet and the other drugs to ameliorate the many symptoms of the disease, yet this was the case before 1960. This must have also increased the dread of PD's progression as well. Back then as well, doctors did not even talk about a possible cure in five years.

Grandma had other burdens. There was a war on back then (World War II–it was in all of the papers) and she had four sons. All went to war. Unlike today, they could not call home every night to check in and they did not take TV crews with them on missions, in fact; they were not allowed to tell anyone where they were.

Ted, the eldest, distinguished himself by earning a battlefield commission for bravery in bloody combat in France and later a Silver Star in Korea. Bob was wounded in Italy. Chuck was a Marine and went ashore the first day (and stayed for the duration) of the bloodiest battle in all of history–Iwo Jima. Jim, the youngest, was still in basic training when the war ended.

And I'm to be put off a little because of a few wrinkles? Am I to be discouraged because my Deep Brain Stimulator cannot be adjusted quickly enough? Would Grandma have gone on "Oprah" and whined about her life?

When the rest of you become depressed and sad, I want you to stick out your chin and pretend you are Iowans and get through it. Oh yeah, and exercise daily.

Buying the Farm an Inch at a Time

It must have been an Iowan who first used the term "buying the farm" as a euphuism for dying. Iowa farmers have a strange sense of humor. It comes from the daily struggle known as farming. A farmer must battle the weather, weeds, bugs, and anything else trying to destroy his crop. Food is not manufactured; it is grown. Manufacturers build their products in a controlled environment, usually inside. Farmers depend on rain and snow in reasonable amounts. I would guess a manufacturer rarely spends his moments with his maker, praying for rain. I would further speculate that if the first request heard in a prayer was for rain or for the rain to stop, God assumes that there is a farmer on the other end.

But I digress. Life itself is, I guess, a degenerative disease that ends in us joining the choir immortal. PD progresses so slowly we can't generally recognize the daily decline. I didn't notice the day I got my 100th grey hair. I do remember the day one of my children, when asked my hair color, answered "grey." This was not what I thought my overall hair color was. Had I been lying to the Drivers License Bureau for years? Is there a form for reporting change of hair color? Ah, the un-jaded eyes of the young. I remember regarding my grandparents when they were my present age as really, really old.

But I digress again. My real point is Parkinson's disease is buying the farm an inch at a time. I notice more often when I get an inch closer to title, free and clear. This weekend my wife said, as we attended a football game which necessitated a lot of walking, that we should buy a wheelchair for such events in the future. She is right, of course, but this seemed as though I was buying a foot or maybe even a yard.

But life is about living, not about dying. My mother often said, "You have to die of something." I agree, but would stipulate that it shouldn't be Parkinson's.

Mom was a true Iowan with all of the fatalism that the honor carries with it. Grandma always excused our coming home filthy from play by saying, "You have to eat a peck of dirt before you die." (If I hadn't eaten so much back then, I'd have a longer life span in front of me.) However, just because you are an Iowan doesn't mean you should ignore out-of-state advice such as "Gather ye rose buds while ye may."

I can't figure out if I've digressed again or not. The point is that you are going to die sooner or later. You have a little say in this, depending on how much you want to fight. God doesn't distribute brains and good looks equally. He does, however, give each of us the same amount of time each day. If you have PD and move slowly, you'll have to be extra careful not to waste it. Time spent with your family is not wasted if the TV is off.

My Three Rules for Dealing With PD

I think time is going by faster and faster as I slow down with this thing called Parkinson's. This is now to the point where I sometimes get confused on dates. In a rush, I looked at the wrong week ahead. I recently goofed in a big way. On September 20th I was supposed to speak at the Westerville Parkinson's Support Group and I didn't show up. This is inexcusable. Here is my excuse. I always write down such commitments in my daily calendar, which I always carry with me. This memory aid has become necessary, due either to advancing age and/or PD. I always check my book by looking at next week's commitments at the end of each week so I can plan with my wife who does what and when.

What does one do after such a gaffe? The answer is to change your system so it won't happen again. Write appointments and notes in an appointment book.

But my real problem is that I have not been following Virginia Phillips' three rules of dealing with PD. Virginia is a care giver and long-time worker for COPS as a support group leader, board member, newsletter feature writer, newsletter folder, and anything-else-that-needed-to-be-done kind of person.

After years of caring for her late husband and dealing with his PD, now Virginia is on the other side. She has been diagnosed with PD.

My father always told me that I should strive in life to be in the company of minds greater than my own. This has been easy for me, thanks to people like Virginia. This is what makes COPS great; the sharing of ideas and tips with those who have "been there, done that, gotten the T-shirt."

Virginia's three rules for those with PD are "Simplify, Simplify, Simplify." Take a moment now and then to think about all you do and decide then to not do those things that no longer make sense. Although Martha Stewart might disagree, life is too short to stuff mushrooms.

Early in life greater minds taught me the value of lists. Keep lists of things that need to be done: birthdays and anniversaries, etc. Assume that you will forget everything and put what you need to remember on a list that is conspicuous.

A final rule I would add is to have fun. You'll not get out of this world alive. I find it better to laugh at things rather than cry. (Note to the Westerville Support Group: I do not mean to imply this rule applies to my no-show at your meeting.)

To summarize, Beetner's (albeit stolen) rules for dealing with PD are Simplify, Keep Lists, and Have Fun. Oh yes, one more–show up when you are supposed to. Do as I say and not as I do.

Hallucinations

My PD has moved forward (down might describe the direction more exactly) another step. I am beginning to experience hallucinations. They do not frighten me as they do for some. For me they are a source of fascination. They began as movement just barely perceived on my periphery and are now moving into my field of vision.

I have heard about people having hallucinations all of my life. I assumed that those who saw such things were crazy and what they saw were some sort of shadowy ghosts. The truth is that I know many PD patients who are sane and complain of hallucinations.

What really amazes me is how detailed they are. When images do not have to be filtered through your eyes, apparently the mind can supply a great deal of clear detail. I know they are not real, but, because of the detail, I cannot resist turning my head for a closer look. When I do, look directly, they vanish. Last week, however, one ran all the way though my field of vision for the first time.

Doctors can often control this phenomenon by adjusting medication and introducing new drugs. I'm not ready for that quite yet. I'm curious about how the hallucinations will develop. They don't speak to me and I don't speak to them so don't be frightened to invite me (or should I say "us?") to your holiday party.

Jell-O™

I grew up in, what seems to me now, another era. My education was fiercely sexist. In the ninth grade in Burlington, Iowa, in the 1950s, a guidance counselor spent five minutes with me to plan my life's work. Their role, as they saw it, was simple–identify the college-bound.

The interview for boys first determined if you had decent grades. If you did, you were placed on the "college track." The next decision point was whether or not you did well in Algebra. If you did, you were placed on the "college-bound technical track." The final decision was that if you displayed little by way of personality, you were assigned engineering. This is how I became an engineer. Never having met a real engineer in my life, I honestly thought, for a while, that I would be driving a train.

What I really wanted to do was to write a newspaper column. When I arrived at Burlington High School and achieved the exalted station in life of a junior, I signed up for journalism. The junior journalism class did the heavy work of actually writing the school newspaper while the seniors supervised and partied.

When the class (25 girls and only three boys) met the first day and the teacher asked us to each fill out a form indicating the aspect of the paper we wanted to be assigned, I proudly asked to be the opinion columnist. I was assigned to the sports page.

I had no abilities in sports, no interest in sports, no knowledge of sports, and because I worked after school, no time to attend the intramural events that would be my beat. I appealed to the teacher. She laid out the facts for me. She only had three boys in the class, and that was barely enough to cover sports. Girls couldn't be expected to do sports, now, could they? She couldn't imagine a boy that didn't love sports. Was something wrong with me?

So my journalism career ended at the end of the semester. I went back to Trigonometry and reading lame columns in the school paper, written by girls, about the importance of school spirit.

As my life turned out, there were other courses I needed. For instance, I should have taken Home Economics. In Iowa in the 1950s no boy ever took Home Ec. Because of my journalism experience, there was already a cloud over my masculinity. Even an attempt to sign up for Home Ec would have resulted in my expulsion from the gym locker room. I didn't even consider it.

Later in life, I suddenly found myself as the sole provider for two children ages 5 and 6. I had to do the cooking and everything else that Home Ec taught. I had zero experience cooking. Outdoor barbequing had yet to appear in Iowa and the unwritten law was that only women were allowed to cook unless you had a chef's license.

My nearest educational training to cooking was Analytical Analysis in Chemistry. There, I was taught the importance of accurately measuring chemicals when doing experiments. ("Experiments" perfectly describe my early cooking.) I would spend five minutes precisely measuring a cup of water the recipe called for. I had no clue about what was involved with anything related to cooking for the most part.

The kids often asked why didn't we have Jell-O like mommy used to make. On Jell-O, I did have knowledge. I remembered hearing my own mother talking to some other women about the difficulties in getting Jell-O to set when pineapple or various other fruits were added. This led me to conclude that Jell-O was reserved for a higher level of the culinary arts than I had obtained, and knew which fruits could be successful in the making of Jell-O.

The children persisted (unaware of my limitations) to the point where, as we passed the Jell-O section of our super market one day, they said, "Dad, there's the Jell-O. Lets get some." Feeling trapped, I picked up a box to see what all was involved in making Jell-O. (There may be male readers who are not aware of the procedure for making Jell-O. If so, they should seat themselves before reading any further.)

One makes Jell-O by dumping the package contents into a bowl, adding one cup of hot water followed by one cup of cold water. Stir. That's it. You're done. I had a college degree, yet I hadn't known how to make Jell-O. Educational reform, it should be noted, has begun, albeit sixty years late.

Why have I taken you this far into my personal life? It was to demonstrate that, had I been able to be in a support group for single males with the custody of children, someone would surely known the truth about Jell-O. Even though 40% of us will become disabled before we meet the grim reaper, we receive absolutely no training in dealing with it, probably not even at a parent's knee. One percent will get PD. I'm sure you never took a class in dealing with PD. How many PD details on the "Jell-O" level are you unaware of?

Look, I've now shared with you my Jell-O recipe, the least you can do is to attend a local support group meeting. I know you'll learn something.

P.S. This column is completely true. You can't make this stuff up.

Sense of Smell

I don't know when my sense of smell left me and don't know if it happened gradually or abruptly. I imagine it happened some time before I was diagnosed with Parkinson's. Recently I read where some researchers believe that loss of smell might be used as an early indicator of the disease.

I thought they told us in school that taste and smell were related. I still have, what seems to me, a good ability to taste things. This might lead you to believe that inability to smell does not constitute a disability or pose any harm. Well, gentle reader, please allow me to disabuse you of that misinformation.

Several years ago, around the Christmas holidays, the family had to leave to do something. There was ice about outside, which meant I could not go with them. I repaired to my office to do some writing. When they did return, they (all women) said there was a strong odor of natural gas in the house. Since I was bereft of my olfactory senses, I hadn't noticed.

I said that I would go outside and turn the main gas valve off. The Mrs. vetoed that idea, based on the ice outside and her perception that Parkinson's had so addled my brain that I might matters worse by turning the wrong thing. Luckily, the man across the street was general manager of a large plumbing company, and my wife dispatched one of the children to fetch him at once. In the meantime, she ordered a mandatory evacuation of the premises. I was, allowing for the ice, ordered to go no further than the front stoop. This showed that she would rather see me dead than injured. At this juncture, I quickly decided this was an inopportune moment to point this out.

Our friend ran over in his slippers and opened every door and window he could find. He then tracked down the source as the fireplace log lighter left ajar. He told my wife that there was so much gas in the house that a spark would have been a catastrophe for my house, my family, and probably some of my neighbors.

The solution for my wife, other than replacing her husband, was to buy a natural gas detector. These are the size of a fire detector and would have sounded the alarm before the situation got so out of hand.

So, you should have a smoke detector (I can't smell burning homes), a carbon monoxide detector (no one can smell this deadly gas), and a natural gas detector. The only other requirement is a hearing aid, if needed.

Learning to Love Prunes

Last year I had the pleasure of speaking to many support groups. We are blessed with groups that are not hesitant to speak up and ask questions. One of the most common questions concerns constipation. Most Parkinsonian's have long ago given up any embarrassment about the subject which causes so much misery and discomfort.

Until last year, I considered myself an expert on the subject. I found that drinking a good-tasting mineral water during the day helped get down the large amount of water we need to stay regular. That, combined with regular exercise and an occasional Colace tablet, kept me in good shape. I even started writing a booklet about dealing with constipation. It was at that point that everything stopped working for me.

There were numerous techniques shared by support group members for dealing with the problem. Examples recommended to me included bee pollen, Sienna tea, and others. Everyone is unique, and what works for one, may not work for another. My problem got so bad I sought out an expert on the subject. Constipation is such a common problem that all doctors deal with patients who have, at least, occasional problems.

At my doctor's suggestion, I began to include prunes in my daily diet along with supplemental fiber. I had never cared much for prunes, but I have learned to love them. My mother (if she didn't believe what I was saying) used to say, "You're full of prunes." I now know it is impossible to be full of prunes. I am not cured, but my current regimen helps. You should not suffer needlessly. There are various treatments available from physicians and you should search for one that works for you.

Concealing Parkinson's and Stress

Today's *New York Times* has an article entitled "Shrouded in Secrecy, Parkinson's Takes Greater Toll." They say it's common for people to conceal their Parkinson's, but hiding the disease may carry consequences. They told of people and their efforts to mask the symptoms. One person was a school secretary who was diagnosed at 45 and kept it mostly to herself for seven years. Of course, it became harder and harder to conceal, causing a great deal of stress in her life.

It was hard to hide shaking hands and her lipstick was very hard to put on straight. "I didn't want anybody to feel sorry for me," she said. "To have people look at you and start crying—that's not what anyone wants."

She now regrets having waited so long. This is all too common. I know that Michael J. Fox concealed his for about ten years because he feared it would end his film career. Friends always notice that something is wrong even though they may not say it. Usually they fear the worst–meaning cancer or such.

Bill Geist, a CBS news commentator, revealed his Parkinson's on a Sunday morning talk show. He had been living with it for a decade, secretly taking dozens of pills a day. If someone noticed his handwriting at a book signing, he would say he was recovering from a broken wrist.

My handwriting is so bad, I can't even read notes I write to myself. This symptom is called micrographia which, is characterized by very small writing that is not straight on the page, as well as difficulty making legible letters due to the gradual loss of small motor skills.

Lastly, a woman who was an OB-GYN in **Cleveland, Ohio (of all places)**, diagnosed at 48, refused to believe it and got the same diagnosis a year later. She did her best to conceal it by slipping into her neurologist's back door. The *New York Times* did not mention if she secretly read my monthly column (you know what egos their writers have).

To her surprise, she found her patients very supportive when she went public with the news. She seized the opportunity to "plunge into fund-raising." Together with her husband, she formed a comedy group called "Shaking with Laughter" to raise money for PD research. I think they went a little too far here. I should have copyrighted PD humor when I had my chance. Had she gone to a support group in her area (Ohio has the most groups of any state), she would have found others to learn from and lean on. It is not too late to join.

Besides making *me* angry, what harm is done by concealing PD? For one, there are research studies under way that are looking for people in the very early stages of PD. A biomarker study, begun in 2010, has recruited just 239 of the 400 patients needed.

In short, if you have PD, admit it, join a support group, and volunteer for any studies underway that may need you. After all, when I was diagnosed in 1994, I went public right away and even gave up my invention called Facebook to write and help others with PD. By rights, I should be the richest man in the universe by now.

Observations

My wife would make a lousy Parkinson's patient. As much as I love her, I will tell you frankly that she has limited skills of observation. She misses many of the details of life.

I first noticed this early in our marriage and have, as I am wont to do, used it to my advantage. An example of this was the time she decided to switch me from butter to margarine in order to bring down my cholesterol level.

I grew up on butter. I love butter. My people were so adamant about butter that the state of Iowa, trying to stem the invasion of margarine, forbade the sale of yellow-colored margarine when I was in my youth.

My wife told me that modern margarines tasted exactly like butter. She bought a pound to prove it. I did not like it, so I bought some real butter on my own. She saw the box in the refrigerator after several weeks and said we were staying with margarine and butter was *not* allowed. Lesser men would have been thrown into abject despair.

I simply continued to buy butter and put the sticks in the margarine box. For several years she never noticed the word "butter" on her "margarine" stick and never thought it curious that a pound of margarine could last several years. (This is a true story. You can't make this stuff up.)

Many years ago I was doing some consulting in Saudi Arabia. In those days the arrival of anyone from the States occasioned a party. At our party I spoke with a number of doctors. They told me of the cultural differences that made their job more difficult. One difference (and I hope you are not eating breakfast as you read this) was the handling of excretory functions.

Saudis are taught to never look back at their stools. Saudi patients cannot answer questions by doctors about such matters because they don't know. Diagnostic information is lost.

One is not born with good observational skills. I know I was not. I did not realize how bad my skills were until I took a walk in the woods with Dick West. In my former life, I did some consulting and one of my clients was the Bureau of Indian Affairs. It was there that I met Mr. West, who was chair of the Art Department at Haskell Indian College.

Dick was a Sioux chief and looked every bit the part, beginning with his body carriage that screamed command. He also had the soft, patient voice and manner that revealed his compassion and interest in nature and his fellow man.

He suggested we go for a walk in the woods as we discussed the facility requirements for his department. We had hardly begun when he observed that it would snow soon. I said it was not in the weather forecast. He said, "See how all of those cows are standing with their behinds pointing to the northwest? They do that when it is going to snow."

Sure enough, it began to snow shortly after that. He proceeded to tell me which animals had passed by this spot recently, how you could tell the severity of the coming winter, and so forth until I felt like a blind man standing next to him. From that moment on, I resolved to be more observant of life.

This is a skill you must develop in order to become a good PD patient. Your problem condition (a bad term but better than "disease") is located in a very inaccessible spot in your body. I'm sure doctors would like to biopsy your brain at every visit to measure the rate of cell death of the dopamine producers. They have to settle for a little snapshot of your life as you appear at that moment.

Many Parkinsonians claim they always seem to be "up" for a doctor visit. In my case, I think there is some truth in that. Anyway, the doctor is very dependent on your observations of how things have been going. If you can identify what causes you to go "off" or what causes more dyskinesia, your doctor will be better able to help.

Finally, always keep track of when you moved your bowels so you know when you are getting into trouble. Unless I miss my guess, Saudi Parkinsonians who do not notice this will die of bowel impaction. Think how that would look in your obit.

Hospital Tip – Don't Get Sick in July

I want to make some suggestions for managing your medical care beyond PD. I am not a doctor, but a lay consumer of those practitioners of the medical arts. Nor am I a lawyer, another learned profession. In fact, lawyers like to point out that while a group of lawyers were drafting the U.S. constitution, widely regarded as the finest bit of legal work the world has seen, doctors were treating George Washington with leeches.

Medicine has come a long way since then, but not to the point where you should abandon your rights and the ultimate decision making on your treatment.

First, a couple of things I've learned in life that may save you some grief. Never schedule surgery for Thursday or Friday. Hospitals are short-handed on weekdays, but nearly abandoned on the week ends. You don't want to be dependent on medical help who are not there.

Next, avoid teaching hospitals during July. That's when medical residents, newly graduated from medical school, start learning how to be doctors, and they learn by taking care of patients. Learning means making mistakes. Hospitals suddenly have some new people in charge of your care with limited experience who are highly-stressed, sleep-deprived, and can't find their way around a strange, new hospital. My third child was born in a New York hospital on a July 4th weekend. In New York this is called a twofer. I know what I am writing about.

Anytime you have a loved one in the hospital who is incapable of presenting a vigorous defense, have someone there to ask the name of each drug being administered and what it is for. Do not assume that just because you alerted someone about contraindicated drugs, that those drugs will not be proffered. Each time a new drug is introduced, watch for allergic reaction. Be assertive with staff and doctors when you sense something is not going well.

Earlier this year I was operated on to repair a hernia. This is an out-patient procedure these days. My body has a hard time metabolizing anesthetics. In this case I had a spinal. Even though my surgery was early in the morning, I was still paralyzed from my navel south at 3:30 in the afternoon, when out-patient recovery closed for the day. The nurses had been urging me for hours to get up, but I couldn't.

The last remaining nurse wanted to go home, so she told my wife to pull the car up and they would wheel me out to the car. My wife said that she would not be able to carry me from the garage into the house and thought I should be admitted to the hospital. The nurse told us that she couldn't do that. Only doctors can admit patients. My wife refused to budge until they found a doctor to admit me.

About 9:30 that night the anesthetic had worn off to the point where I had gained several more inches of feeling. This exposed to me that I had not emptied my bladder since early that morning and the pain of my distended bladder was severe. I still had no control in that area, so I rang for the nurse. After ringing a third time, she appeared. I explained the situation and asked to be catheterized. No-can-do without a doctor's order. Could she call a doctor? Well, it was a bit late. I insisted.

A half hour passed and I rang again. They were still waiting for an order. I knew that you could die from a burst bladder. I thought about calling 911 and requesting transportation from my hospital room to a nearby emergency room.

To add a bit of irony here, the cover of this hospital's last annual report has a picture of a family strolling across a green meadow hand-in-hand, with their arms raised in apparent jubilation. I know because that is me and my family. I began to compose a press release to be issued upon of my demise later that evening. To assure front-page treatment by the media, I headlined it "Local Hospital Kills Its Own Cover Boy." I described myself as a local luminary whose life's record was besmirched only by his mother's traffic conviction.

Seconds before my forced exit from this veil of tears, the order came through. My revenge was sweet. The nurses, who thought I was just being a baby, did not bring a container large enough for the bounty they received.

I hereby swear/affirm that every word in this column is the truth. You can't make this stuff up.

A Short Essay on Time

There are two types of time in this world. One I'll call real-world time and the other Parkinson's or PD time. Each PD patient has their own version of PD time. For example, getting dressed in the morning takes me 10 minutes which, translates to 15 minutes real-world time. There are two PD symptoms that slow us down: 1) slowness of movement, 2) rigidity, and 3) tremor. Make that three symptoms.

Doctors, airplanes, and schools run on real-world time, although doctors are usually in a later time zone. The point I want to make is–recognize that you are in a different time space than the non-PD world and allow yourself more time to do things.

God gives everyone the same 24-hour allotment of time everyday. Even if you didn't take a differential equations course in college, you realize you can't get as much done now as you used to. Your first step toward having more time is to simplify your life. There are things you do that don't need to be done. Although I've read the *Wall Street Journal* for years, I'm not renewing my subscription. I found that I was reading it partly out of habit, not out of necessity. I found a responsible adult (investment advisor) to take charge of my investments. Owing to their size, this is not a big job for him, but saves me time.

Another peculiarity of PD time is the "The Parkinson Cure is About Five Years Away" rule. I have been hearing this for the past eleven years. Researchers *are* making progress. On the plus side, there are new drugs coming to market aimed at relieving symptoms–not as a cure. Sinemet, the first neurological drug to treat PD patients in a wide-spread fashion, was released in 1970. Given the number of drugs available today and the 2000+ years of people with PD, we are starting to make some progress.

What I think may happen is that a PD cure may take the same path as our conquest of polio. Polio no longer threatens our children as it did when I was in grade school. The Polio vaccine protects against the recipient from contracting the disease. We claim then to have conquered polio but, it was not an unconditional surrender. Polio got to keep all that were already infected.

It may be different for us. Remember that when diagnosed with PD, you have actually had PD for a long time before that diagnosis. Your body had been compensating for the lack of dopamine until it could no longer keep up. Only after about 70% of the dopamine-producing neurons stopped working did symptoms appear. While it wouldn't be a cure in the true sense of the word, if they can just reactivate enough neurons to get us back over the 70% barrier, we would be back to the symptom-free side.

There is hope because there are a number of researchers working on studies that could become restorative steps. While that goes on, you should keep your body ready. Scientists are now beginning to believe that exercise is a neuro-protector and you don't need a doctor's prescription for that.

It also pays to be optimistic. My mother always was and anytime someone was thinking about the end, she would always say something like, "Don't talk like that. You'll live to be a hundred." Mom always operated a beauty shop in our home. She had a faithful list of ladies who became her friends over the many years she did hair. As an example, she was still working when she died at age 86, leaving one woman who had an almost fifty-year standing Friday-appointment.

I recall her calling me into the shop one day to meet her friend May. May was just about to turn 99 and was getting her hair done because she was taking the first airplane trip of her life to visit her great-grandson and his wife in Minneapolis. She told us how excited she was to make the trip, how she had always wanted to fly, and that she was going now because she didn't have much time left. Mom automatically said, "Oh May, you'll live to be a hundred."

That comment hung in the air for a moment while everyone thought about it. It was almost as if she had said, "I wouldn't buy any two-year magazine subscriptions." May did make it to 100.

Driving With Mr. Parkinson

I've had a driver's license since the birthday I became eligible. I won't bore you with how old I was then because what is important is now.

I wrote a column many years ago about knowing when to *stop* driving. Driving, and the independence that comes with it, is hard to give up. Sadly, most of us won't give up until we have an accident. In her eighties, my mother drove in front of an oncoming car she did not see and had her accident. The family gave a sigh of relief that she was not injured. We thought she would stop driving without our having to tell her she should stop. After a month without a car, she went and bought another without conferring with me or my brother. She drove to church and the grocery store for many more years and died with a current license.

Dad, on the other hand, developed dementia. He drove until one day he was unable to explain to a policeman why he was driving the wrong way on the freeway. Thank goodness it was Iowa and there was little traffic. By the time the police arrived, he had pulled off to the side and was sitting there trying to figure out what to do next. In exchange for his license and a promise to never drive again, he was allowed to return to society with his driving record unblemished.

Then came me, by this time the patriarch of the family, and my turn for an accident. Again, lucky for the rest of the world of driving, my first accident was in my own garage. I made the very common mistake of hitting the gas when I meant to hit the brake as I entered my garage. Now, to me, a collision in one's own garage did not seem to imperil anyone since no one else was driving in my garage that day. But that was the beginning of the end.

I only used the car to drive to therapy twice a week, but after the pulmonary embolism episode, everyone grew nervous about my breaking a hip or bleeding to death from a minor cut. I gave up driving but retained the car, which I thought I could perhaps grow into again. Faced with the state of North Carolina wanting me, their newest resident, to take a driving test in order to qualify for a North Carolina driver's license, I demurred. I figured that hiding my driving shortfalls from an examiner would be tougher than hiding daylight from a rooster.

Acting quickly, my family sold my car and bought me an electric golf cart (13 mph downhill with a tail wind) to drive around the neighborhood. The ironic thing is that many of the people in my neighborhood are professional drivers. In my town they teach how to get gasoline and have all four tires replaced in about 11 seconds. Of course, I'm speaking of NASCAR drivers (200 mph just to qualify to race) who make only left turns and learn to avoid accidents by learning to drive through disintegrating cars spinning around them. They call Mooresville, N.C. "Race City USA" for a reason.

I'm lucky that my wife, Sandy, is willing to drive me to doctor's appointments, etc. The only downside is I can't buy her a present on my own to surprise her. The tipoff to her is when I want to go to the local pawn shop. This aside, I hope you can find a solution to your driving problem without an accident before you give neighbors a good laugh as you drive by.

When Two Saints Collide

Several readers took my last month's column to be my final opus. I still have until the end of the year in my term of office. Those who have been kind enough to write in, have said they like my writings about Iowa (or their "home state" as they called it). I'm nothing if not eager to please.

Speaking of saints, having grown up in Iowa, I came to know several. Although the Presbyterian Church does not investigate individuals for evidence of saintliness nor investigate post-mortem miracles, Iowans have the ability to spot saints early. People in Iowa will say things like "that woman is a saint" even though the woman is still alive.

I once observed two saints at cross purposes. One of them was my Great Aunt Bessie. Bessie was born profoundly hard of hearing and, therefore, by the standards of the times not marriageable. Though a good hardworking, God–fearing woman, she never married. Family took care of family and she lived with her younger brother Herd. They were farmers, as was about everyone in Iowa at the time. They worked for years, building up the farm. In those days, you were really tied to your farm. If you had pigs (and who didn't?), you could never spend more than three or four hours away from the farm. But then, that was fine, with only church on Sunday and shopping on Saturday necessitating any absence.

As Uncle Herd rounded 75, a young woman of 34 from church fell in love with him. It was curious that a young woman would fall in love with a man of his advanced age, especially given that he was practically deaf himself, blind in one eye, had a wooden leg, and I think he was missing a finger or two, as was the custom at the time, the price paid to unclog the corn picker without having to shut it down first.

After the wedding, Bessie moved from the family farm where she had lived her entire life to experience life in the city. The city, in this case, was Montrose, Iowa. There were probably as many as 200 people living there at the time. Her sister Gladys, my grandmother, found her a house to rent about a block from her. Montrose was about four blocks square and Grandma didn't want Bessie way over on the other side of town.

Bessie had never been employed as such. She worked very hard on the farm every day of her life. I remember visiting them at the farm and being impressed that the kitchen sink was really neat because the water faucet was a hand pump from the well. They had built the sink directly over the well and then built the house around the sink. They did have electricity, but I don't recall a phone, given that neither one could hear well enough to use it. The electricity allowed them to buy a deep freezer that eliminated the trips to the locker plant in town.

But, as I say, she never joined Social Security, so she had no retirement income. The Presbyterian Church did step up to a monthly pension for her, but it amounted to only $36 a month. She apparently also had some very meager savings.

Herd passed away a couple of years later. No one was surprised to learn that he left the farm and all of his earthly possessions to his bereaved widow. Bessie never even considered challenging the will or to even think ill of Herd.

The second saint in this story was my mother. She would continually check on Bessie. We could tell Bessie was having trouble making ends meet because she stopped buying hearing aid batteries. Part of the problem was that every time we visited, we found another cat or two added to her collection of strays. She was feeding the cats before she bought for herself. Mom suggested she get rid of some of the cats or at least stop adopting every one that came to her door. She demurred, saying she had no choice, given the alternative of cat starvation.

Bessie would not accept charity herself, saying that there were many others needing more help than she. Grandma, after being refused on her proffers of cash, would leave change and small bills around Bessie's house when she was not looking and Bessie would think it was her money that she had forgotten to put away.

Mom was more direct. She gave Bessie $300 over her objections. The following week, Mom read in the church bulletin a 'thank you' to Bessie for her $300 contribution. Determined to help Bessie, Mom took a different tack. To keep Bessie from spending her money on cat food or donating it to the church, Mom went to the store and bought a big supply of staples such as flour, sugar, and butter.

The next church bulletin thanked Bessie for her contribution of 'an extraordinary' donation of cookies and such to the Women's Bake Sale. A woman bound for sainthood cannot be derailed – not even by another saint.

Americans are a very generous people, as evidenced by the outpouring of funds after September 11. Like Bessie, people do not have an endless supply of money for charity. There is great concern among small charities such as COPS that contributions to us will be way down as America reacts to the national disaster.

We'll follow Bessie's example and accept things as they are and continue on our mission to the maximum extent we can.

How to Exercise With Young Women

As the country's foremost male monthly columnist on all things Parkinsonian, I enjoy hearing from readers. Last month I chanced upon a relatively new reader who was diagnosed about three years ago. I asked whether the reader found my column at all helpful. The reply was that what was needed was information about the day-to-day problems in dealing with PD, such as constipation and falling, and not what passed as humor years ago.

I remember writing on these topics in about March of 1997. However, this reader is correct and I shall revisit these topics in future columns.

Before I do, I must clear my inbox of outstanding items. A recently completed study showed that dance helped those with Parkinson's. Actually, many years ago when I was president of COPS, a fellow from Brooklyn wrote me several times, reporting that he had found that tap dancing had slowed the progression of PD and urged me to publicize this to the world. I am embarrassed to admit that I gave his report very little credence. I guess he was on to something. COPS has very generously offered free classes in exercise, voice training, Tai Chi, and the Alexander technique because each has been determined to be of value in PD. Now the society will have to determine if it has the resources to offer tap dance.

There is another form of exercise that I use and find very effective, albeit I know of no research to support or disprove its benefits. It is called Pilates. I had never heard of it before my daughter in Chicago gave me a DVD of beginning Pilates. Pilates concentrates on building core strength, which is my most urgent medical need because of a previous spinal cord injury and a curvature of my spine.

I take three one-hour sessions per week with an instructor. I combine this with a bicycle (actually a tricycle) ride on the other days. Between the two forms of exercise, I think I am making great progress. Pilates is hard work. They say if you don't feel that they are hard work, you are not doing them correctly. I would add that Pilates is the most exercise you can get with your clothes on.

There are classes in Pilates given at various spots around town and there are countless DVDs showing how one can strengthen abs if you are a young, thin woman with incredible flexibility. This explains why I could not do a single exercise on the DVD I was given.

The only other problem I should mention relates to the clientele of a Pilates studio. I am the only male presently enrolled. They in no way discriminate against men. Either men do not like exercises in which women excel or it is not regarded as a manly endeavor. Fortunately, I am secure enough in my sexuality that I can be seen both in Pilates and riding my three-wheeled recumbent bicycle. I'm not sure but I think this speaks well for my character. I could be wrong.

Why Me Lord?

Most of us parkies are diagnosed as "idiopathic Parkinson's" which means Parkinson's Disease of unknown origin. There is nothing science knows of that you could have done to prevent PD – save possibly smoking. There *have* been studies that found an inverse correlation between smoking and PD. Had you chosen to smoke, you'd probably have something worse by now.

That being said, we all went home from the doctor's office that fateful day of diagnosis and said, "Why me, Lord?" Actually, that's not true. Many go home from the doctor's office saying, "That's wrong. It can't be true." This is called denial and some professionals say we all go through this stage to some extent. It's later that we say "Why me?"

I've read a couple of books on the "Why me" subject and still had not found a satisfactory answer until yesterday.

My sainted mother always told me, "God never gives you greater burdens than you can carry." I figured that God had misjudged me. My particular burdens began with a skiing accident that injured my spinal cord. It left me quadriplegic. Months of physical therapy got me walking again, at which point, PD was added to my burdens.

From then on, my burdens seemed to grow at a rate that would have amazed even Job.

Job certainly had his problems such as a plague of locusts. I would gladly trade the plague of personal computer problems enveloping me in recent years for a million grasshoppers.

Last month (both of my regular readers may have noticed), I did not write my regular column. This was because my two newest burdens were spinal surgery and the sudden passing of my mother. Mom must have been right about the number of burdens because I am still here. (Please Lord do not take this as an invitation for more.)

But, as I sat thinking about what I could have done to deserve all of this, I wondered, "Why is God testing me like this?" Then it came to me. Obviously I am being considered for a high position in the hereafter and I am undergoing testing here on earth.

Parkinson's and Trump's Hair

Parkinson's is sometimes called a "designer" disease because it has so many symptoms, any or all of which may be present in a patient. Complicating the matter, other diseases or problems may exacerbate the symptoms even more. I know I do not have to tell you about the aging process and what it does to the mind and body.

If you, like me, have PD, I'm sure there are some symptoms that bother you more than others. The one I hate the most came with my Deep Brain Surgery (DBS). What it does is to cause my voice to show much more feeling than I really feel. For example, if I tell someone about reading in the paper that a plane crashed in Outer Magnolia my voice wavers and cracks as if I knew everyone onboard. I choke up and many people cannot understand what I am saying.

I researched the problem (that is "Googled" it). I learned that the section of brain that controls body movements also controls some emotions. Hence, my over-reaction to sadness.

It is very embarrassing to be at a party talking with people and, let's say, that Donald Trump's hair comes up. As I start to express my feelings, it sounds to the others that they somehow stumbled into an area of deep sadness for me. My listeners feel uncomfortable and immediately try and change the subject.

I can only imagine the conversations other people have about it on the way home.

"Did you see the way Michael reacted to the discussion of Donald Trump's hair? What was that all about?"

"He always was a little weird."

"Which one–Beetner or Trump?"

"Both."

While this may not seem like much to you, it really does embarrass me. I'm sure there is not a researcher in a lab somewhere working on the problem. The researcher would have to design a very small DBS unit that would fit on a fruit fly, implant it, and then engage him in a discussion of Trump's hair. Your average fruit fly would have little interest in Trump's hair other than as a possible nesting area.

Enough is Enough

My PD was diagnosed in December of 1994. There hasn't been a day since then that the disease didn't remind me of its presence. For several years after that (especially during my early years at COPS), I believed researchers when they said the cure for PD was only about five years away. I spoke optimistically about the honor I would have closing down COPS after the cure was administered to our members.

I remember reporting on fetal pig brain implants. The thought was that pieces of brain matter from pig embryos could be implanted in the human brain and these implants could restore dopamine production. I contacted one of the patients in that research study who had undergone implant surgery. He graciously wrote several articles for this newsletter describing his improvement.

At this point I feel obligated to pause and assure you, dear reader, that I am not making this up. Pigs have been used for many years to provide heart valves for humans. Pigs have a close fit with human genetic material. Add to this the fact that the human brain is immunio-priveldged which means the brain does not try to use bodily defenses to kill the implant, always a problem elsewhere in the body. It didn't work for some reason and the study was discontinued.

I remember at least three times when a group of PD researchers announced that they had found the "Parkinson gene" that triggered the disease. They, as it turns out, had found "a" gene, not "the" gene.

The next great hope was the stem cell. Invariably, journalists, when writing of the promises of stem cells, describe stem cells as a potential cure for Parkinson's. Many even ventured that PD would be the first condition to be cured by stem cells. But, it hasn't happened.

Flash forward to today. *The New York Times* science section has a report from researchers who have found that teaching those with PD to tango, greatly improves their ability to move and improves balance. Well, I'm old and tired and don't want to take dance lessons with a bunch of senior citizens prone to falling down. Going back to the *Times* story, it ended as do all research articles with the caution that additional research in this area is needed. The obvious implication is that the group would like more money to study this further.

Parkinson's has interfered with my life every single day since 1994. PD has long past being "fun" and doing the tango seems to be on a par with treatments by atomic mole people.

If any of you try tangoing to a cure, please let us know how you are doing. It would be just my luck to stop one step short of a cure.

Depression

Doctors say that it is impossible to diagnose depression in an Iowan. Newscasts on the radio in Iowa include the prices being paid for corn, soybeans, and hogs. A good crop means oversupply and prices so low it doesn't pay for the seed and fertilizer. The price goes up when the crop is bad but you don't have enough to sell to cover costs. A happy farmer in Iowa is one who is still in denial.

Depression is quite common in Parkinson's patients. Some estimates are as high as 60% will have some symptoms of depression. Depression keeps you from enjoying life and getting things done. We don't need that.

Fortunately, there are treatments for it. You should see a neurologist about depression. Lucky you, you are probably already seeing one. The anti-depressant drugs really work. They do not, as I had always supposed, turn you into either a vegetable or a smiling idiot. They merely raise your spirits enough to see that life is funny.

If you are reluctant to take the step of taking a drug specifically for depression, you might try one of the dopamine agonists such as Mirapex® that have a mood elevation side effect.

I'm not done with you yet on this subject. After you conquer your depression either by medicine or show girls, you must remember it is your duty to provide feedback to those around you that you are no longer depressed. Parkinson's gets in your way by diminishing your facial expressions so you will have to make conscious efforts to smile.

A Brief History of Parkinson's Treatment

An ancient civilization in India practiced a medical doctrine called Ayarveda. It is claimed that Ayarveda was the divine revelation of the creator God Lord Brahma as he awoke to create the universe. The symptoms of PD (which they called Kampavata) were described as far back as 5000 BC. To treat the disease they used a tropical legume called Mucuna Pruriens. Mucuna Pruriens' seeds are a natural source of therapeutic quantities of L-dopa which is used today as the gold standard of PD treatment.

In the 1950's L-Dopa was rediscovered for symptomatic treatment of Parkinson's. Guess the source for L-Dopa—Macuna Pruriens seeds. The researcher responsible, Arvid Carlsson, was awarded the Nobel Prize in medicine in the year 2000. No rush here. As long as I have had PD, the cure has always been five years away. I can only believe that it was such back to 5000 BC. Researchers took almost 7,000 years to return us to what they were using way back then.

There was that brief moment a few years ago when we felt we could do anything. After all, we put a man on the moon and put a stop to polio. Polio was never cured as popular legend has it (we only prevented future cases). At this point in history we got a little full of ourselves and President Nixon declared "war" on cancer. Over the years we spent over $200 billion dollars on this quest. We lost the war.

I'll bet that 7,010 years ago they were collecting gold for further Kampavata research which they said would lead to a cure in five years. I only know I have been diagnosed for fifteen years and every year have been told the cure was only about five years away. Gosh, can it be that they are wrong?

What is going wrong? Permit me a couple of modest examples. Researchers have found that even small amounts of the element manganese have been related to PD. Manganese is present in the drinking water of many Americans. What limits does the EPA set for manganese in our water? None—that's right, they have no limits. What good is research if we do not apply its findings?

Since I'm on a rant now, let me get more off my chest. I am currently trying a Pilates exercise routine to improve my balance and core strength. Recently I found a research report titled "Effectiveness of Pilates in the Reduction of Fear of Falling with Parkinson's Disease: A Case Report." This report was written at the University of Miami, Coral Gables, Florida. It credits six authors.

There are many components to look for in a good study; chief among them carefully selected treatment and control groups of adequate size. This study did not have a control group. The treatment group consisted of one person. This is not a typo—one (1) person. This person was an 84 year-old man who had difficulty staying awake and following commands and simple instructions. This is hardly the typical PD patient.

I don't think any researcher truly interested in doing anything other than add a published paper to his or her resume would even sign their name to this. Someone authorized money to be spent on PD research and this is what we get.

In summary, we do some research that shouldn't even be called research and when we do have a bit of research that shows something that contributes to our developing PD, we ignore it. No wonder 7,010 years have gone by without finding a cure. Or perhaps a cure was found, say 6,000 years ago and needs to be found again.

Let's become active about this kind of nonsense and not wait another 7,010 years. Frankly, I don't think I can hold on that long. Besides, this disease is keeping me from finishing my life's work of developing removable underwear.

The Column I've Always Wanted To Write

Your humble narrator has often spoken in this very column of his certainty that a cure is in our future. There have been many detractors that doubted we would see any such cure during our lifetime. Indeed, even I harbored some doubts.

I am not your typical Parkinsonian (if there is such a thing). Four years prior to my diagnosis, I had a serious skiing accident that injured my spinal cord. Like PD, there is no present cure for this.

This month brings news that drug trials will begin later this year on a new drug which is believed to be a "restorative." This drug is a neural growth factor which promises to re-grow dopamine producing cells. Even better, it may also grow new nerve cells to help my spinal cord injury. It is as if I won the lottery.

First things first. What is the difference between a "restorative" and a "cure?" It always seemed to me that if you restored the brain's dopamine producing capability, you cured PD. I queried my neurologist on the difference.

A cure is something that cures the problem completely to the point that one cannot tell that the subject ever had the problem. Researchers are not prepared to claim a cure at this early stage of this new drug. It may be that the newly generated cells will, in turn, be attacked by whatever causes

PD to begin with and we will have to continue to take this medicine for the rest of our life.

While such an outcome is not a cure, restoration of bodily function and elimination of PD symptoms is enough for me. This will make waiting for the cure a snap.

Before you stop reading to get in line at your neurologist's office, let's be clear just where this drug stands. (Incidentally, the line forms directly behind me.) The drug, GPI-1046, is expected to enter human trials later this year. It has passed primate testing; now it must be determined if it works with humans. These tests are always conducted as "double blind," meaning that half of the volunteers receive the drug and the other half receives a placebo. Neither patient nor administering physician know which is being given.

There may also be bad side effects that testing to date that has not yet surfaced. It takes a long time for a drug to be approved even after successful trials. But there is always hope.

This hope should kick your exercise program into high gear. You can't just sit and await the cure and expect that your body will be in good enough shape when your turn comes up.

Finally, I said earlier in this column that this new drug that could solve both of my problems was just like winning the lottery. It so happens that I did win a million dollars in the Iowa lottery this past month. The Iowa lottery is different than most—it pays out at a dollar a year for a million years.

Post Script: After the column above had been written I learned that I do not qualify for participation because I have had PD for more than five years and have motor fluctuations.

On the bright side, the study is only six months long. They must expect to see improvement in that short of time!

Sex vs. PD

This month's topic is sex. This is always a difficult subject to discuss in public and support groups seldom venture into this territory. Physicians note that "sexual difficulties" is one of the multitude of possible PD symptoms. Lack of open discussion leaves us often confused about whether a problem is merely a function of normal aging and what is a treatable condition. Researchers now tell us that someday people will be able to continue their sex lives until well into their fifties.

I can find no books dealing solely with sex and PD. Such a book, while not a best-seller, would, no doubt, out-sell a book about PD and humor, but this is faint praise as I can testify.

Polite conversation is always "save you and I," so why is there so little discussion of this topic? Nightly we see TV commercials dealing with erectile dysfunction (ED), urinary problems, hemorrhoids, and political candidates for public office. Why are we not offended? The answer, I suspect, is the "Parkinson personality" I have written about before.

My review of the literature on sexuality and PD reveals a modest number of studies about the various drugs and devices used in the management of PD. The vast majority of the studies are about men. Female sexual dysfunction in PD is what scientists call "poorly researched." Naturally, most of the studies center on erectile dysfunction (ED). Too much attention is paid to ED thanks, in recent years, to drug companies.

Dr. George Paulson, known to many of you for his many years of work in PD and his contributions to our newsletter, wrote "There are many ways to express love and intimacy." This is important. Love is not about one act. A PD patient has many strikes against them to begin with–difficulty moving in bed, off-periods, difficulty with fine body movement, among others. We worry that our sex appeal is diminished by symptoms such as drooling. The challenge is to not let PD dictate your love life. A simple "I love you" and hugs go a long way for both patient and caregiver.

One other hint for strengthening a relationship comes from my mother who always said "Flattery will get you everywhere with me." I think that is true of either sex. (Readers will note that I did not write "I think this is true of either *gender*" as most modern writers are wont to do. Substituting gender for sex and verbal for oral destroys the meaning of each. But, I digress.)

Drugs prescribed for PD symptoms often play an important role in both reducing libido and increasing ED. Watch for new troubles of any sort when your medication changes and do not be timid about telling your physician. You will not shock your doctor.

As far as ED is concerned, urologists say that it is now 100% treatable. Unless you never watch TV or read a magazine, you know that there are three competing drugs (Viagra, Cialis, and Levitra) on the market by prescription. If these do not work, there are older drug treatments that may. Failing all else, there are devices that can be implanted in the penis to mechanically inflate it.

One last warning in the other direction – rarely some drugs, especially Sinemet, may cause hyper sexuality which is defined as, "a fixation on sexuality with the development of a ravenous sexual appetite."

I would be remiss if I concluded this topic without an Iowa story. An Iowa farm couple was discussing finances when the subject of Buster, their prize-wining bull, came up. The wife asked how many times Buster stood at stud last year. The man replied, "About 200." "Too bad you are not like Buster," she said pointedly. He ended the conversation by pointing out that all 200 were not with the same cow.

Hearing Aids

The electronic digital computer was invented during my lifetime. Although there were competing claims from different inventors, the courts finally decided that the first electronic digital computer was invented by John Vincent Atanasoff, a physics and math professor at Iowa State University. I first became aware of computers when I read an article in *Popular Mechanics* magazine in 1956. The author of the article described electric brains capable of doing the work of twenty mathematicians without ever making a single error. Further, these electric brains could be set to work seven days a week and never require time off.

Iowans, by nature, are technology freaks. If you don't believe me just take a close look at power farm machinery. The average farm combine has more computer power than the space shuttle. While I was technically not a farm boy, even a "city boy" living in Iowa can never be more than 2.1 miles from a farm. I decided that my future would be in electric brains.

I attended the University of Iowa (different than Iowa State) because it was a rarity at the time–it allowed students to use the computer. I took every computer class on campus (one). It was called Programming Digital Computers. This is how I became an early "geek." Bill Gates was still in grade school.

The two controllers for my deep brain stimulators probably exceed the computing power of the entire world when I started work. Well, flash forward to today. My own (non-electric) brain has had some circuits go bad and my hearing has also gone south.

Of course hearing aids have gone high tech and are now digital. The Iowan in me read the ads about how these devices are small enough to hide in the ear so that no one will ever know I have them. Vanity is not unknown in Iowans and I thought this would be a wonderful technological solution to my hearing problem.

I should acknowledge that my hearing has been lacking the higher frequencies for some time. This results in the inability to hear the consonants needed to understand speech. Oh, I tried to compensate by living in states like Iowa and Ohio where the name of the state used only minimal consonants – but this was not enough.

Recently I took my eagerness for technology along with my vanity to buy hearing aids. The same way an Iowan farmer buys a tractor, I picked out the smallest, least visible model with all of the extras such as telephone compatibility, directional microphones, seven levels of frequency compensation, and up to four different programs to suit the special environment (such as a restaurant) where noise is a big problem.

Hearing aids are not sold by the pound. This is because they would be about $65,000 per pound and that would make even an Iowan think twice.

It took a week from taking a mold of my ear canal until my custom-fitted, completely-in-the-ear-canal aids were ready. If you have had DBS surgery, you know that a wire runs from the controllers in your chest to the top of your head via the clearing directly behind your ear. The hearing aids can "talk" to each other by radio signals so there is a possible problem of your deep brain stimulators picking up your enhanced consonants and using them to fry your brain. *Therefore, it is imperative that you check with your DBS maker to be certain you can use the specific hearing aid with the model DBS unit you have.*

My experience with hearing aids was dismal. You have 12 seconds to put both units in your ears before they turn on and provide a feedback in your ears close to the feedback whine experienced as the announcer introduces a rock band to an auditorium of teenagers. PD has stolen much of my manual dexterity and also slowed my movements to the point where I will never be able to insert them that quickly.

Other than that, because they are plastic and fit completely in the ear canal, they feel to the user like globs of plastic plugging his ears. They also warned me that I would be entering a "noisy" world that may take some getting used to. On the way out the door I was deafened by birds cheeping. Opening a sandwich bag could be mistaken for the beginning of WW3. I had not realized that restaurants have someone banging dishes together to drown out the Muzak.

All hearing aids come with a 30-day return policy which I used to get some behind-the-ear units which are somewhat better. But be forewarned, if you notice them and ask "What kind is it?" I am liable to answer with something like "About 1:30."

The Beetner Cure

Before the FDA approves a new drug, the manufacturer must place the drug in double-blind trials. A double-blind study is one where neither the patient nor the attending physician know if the patient is getting the real drug or a placebo. This is necessary to counteract the "placebo effect" which occurs when the patients get better because they think they are taking an effective drug. Often something like 20% of the control or placebo group experience a benefit from the placebo. The improvement is very real as verified by the doctor – it is just not really due to the drug.

Unlike the other small-thinkers developing drugs to treat a symptom or two, I have developed a placebo that is a "cure" for PD. If 20% who take it experience a cure then we will have saved a lot of people. Placebos are just sugar pills and are therefore cheap to make. So there you have it – a cheap cure for PD. It only cures 20% but that is a better cure rate than anybody else has accomplished at this point.

After the Cure

Sometimes, as I read drug company press releases, it seems as if every researcher is working on a cure for PD. There are so many approaches under way that one will surely bear fruit. As I dream about the post-PD world, I foresee problems. Foremost is the problem of retraining those neurologists that are dedicated to PD. The idea of meeting my neurologist at the McDonald's window or selling pencils on the street corner is disturbing.

I think they are best suited to become airline desk agents because they have had vast experience dealing with people who have been waiting for a long time.

The Parkinson Personality

It has been long noted by Parkinson's researchers that the preponderance of patients are "morally resolute," "cautious," and "uninterested in seeking out new experiences." In fact, Dr. James Parkinson, in his treatise that provided the description of the "disease" that has come to bear his name, referred to the first patient he described as a humble gardener who led a life of "remarkable temperament and sobriety."

The list of notables afflicted include the late Pope John Paul II, the Rev. Billy Graham, Muhammad Ali (remember when his religious beliefs ran contrary to the Vietnam War), former Attorney General Janet Reno, Michael J. Fox (one wife, nice family, not part of the Hollywood culture), and me. There are others.

In fact, there are studies that show drinking alcohol and smoking have a reverse correlation to PD. I have met more than a few people with PD in my life and not found a scoundrel among them. I *did* note a number with ego problems.

Some historians think that Hitler and Franco of Spain had PD. The CIA thinks Fidel Castro has PD. There is no proof of any of this and I never met any of them, so we will disregard this group.

A new study, just completed in England, Australia, and Holland confirms that PD patients were less likely to have smoked and drank less coffee and alcohol than their non-PD cohorts. They also found a correlation between less risk-taking and sensation-seeking behavior with PD. This is because people with Parkinson's tend to spurn openly hedonistic activity, while being scrupulous, socially withdrawn and disinclined to take risks.

There are anatomical reasons for our behavior. I am not a neurologist but have employed them for years. They point out that dopamine (which we lack in the mid-brain for motor control) is used as a natural reward mechanism elsewhere in the brain. There it controls how we define pleasure. A gambler gets a dopamine rush when he places a large bet. PD patients, who gradually lose dopamine, have a natural aversion to these types of sensations.

An estimated 5% of PD patients treated with drug therapy exhibit a range of new symptoms which the neurologists call "unsettling characteristics." They can be minor, such as a person who now buys a lottery ticket, or can be serious. Serious behavior problems include extensive gambling, overeating and obsessive compulsive disorders. These may also include addiction and making inappropriate sexual advances. These same drugs make the remaining 95% of us constipated.

Care givers should be fore warned so they can report any personality changes to the neurologist. The solution may be as simple as changing from a dopamine-boosting drug to an agonist or other medicine change. Only your doctor can help. Anyway, the brain is my second favorite body part.

Getting back to the general PD personality, it does have some downsides. We are not the type to attend congressional hearings banging pots and pans until our research funds are increased. This is why the funding for PD research per patient is so much less than the pot-banger's causes.

Then there is the ego problem I referred to earlier. Large egos are primarily seen in Parkinson leaders. Ego problems are, in part, responsible for the divided front in the struggle with PD. Rather than have a single voice such as The American Cancer Society or The American Heart Association, we have The National Parkinson Foundation, The American Parkinson's Disease Association, Parkinson's Disease Foundation, the Michael J. Fox Foundation for Parkinson's Research, the Parkinson's Action Network, and the Parkinson Alliance.

There have been merger talks from time-to-time, but no mergers. People are reluctant to give up their kingdoms. These Parkinson leaders are to humbleness what Paris Hilton is to modesty.

I suppose some sort of summary is in order. First, you are in good company if you have PD. Second, if you see one of us doing something out of character, it's probably the medication talking. Third, if you really want to avoid PD in your children, you can encourage them to drink, smoke, and engage in risky behaviors or you can get out your pots and pans and help get more funding for a cure. It's up to you.

Establish Rules for the Use of Your Brain

The Cleveland Clinic calls the Neurology/Neurosurgery Department the "Center for Neurological Restoration." This always seemed a little grandiose to me but I always hoped it was something they could grow into. Now, they are looking for volunteers for a new study in which a Neurturin gene is implanted in the brain. Previous studies have shown that this will stop the progression of idiopathic PD (Parkinson's of unknown causes).

All I really know about this study is what I have read from their press release. The study coordinator is the woman I see at the clinic for my DBS. I was there just a few weeks ago and she did not mention this to me and I see that DBS patients are ineligible. So, what follows is written completely based on this press release. As always, our newsletter does not recommend any specific medical provider.

If you are thinking of volunteering, first of all, God bless you. Second, your volunteering need not be 100% altruistic. There are some things you should know in advance and there are other points you should insist upon. From the press release it seems as though this is a late stage study of efficacy (does it really work) in humans prior to FDA approval. Previous steps have shown it to work in animal models and another step has shown that it appears to be safe to implant in human brains.

Before volunteering, here are the points I would want to know and the conditions I would impose on the Clinic. First, you should realize that this is a double-blind study. This means that you will have only a 50-50 chance that they will actually implant the Neurturin in your brain. You will not know until the end of the study (up to 19 months) if you even received the drug. There is a risk associated with any surgery and you may be taking the risk of even dying and still have no benefit. In fact, even if you do get the drug, it may not be effective.

You should also remember that this is a neuroprotective, not a cure. This means it will only halt the disease at your present level so it is not a cure meaning you won't get better. Don't get me wrong, I am all in favor of that but your expectations must be not exaggerated.

I would also assume (but you should check) that if you are in the control or non-treatment group that your sham surgery consists of only cutting the scalp and perhaps drilling only a partial hole through the skull to minimize the possible surgical complications yet not tip off doctors evaluating the drug.

It is common, and you should insist, that here be a clause in your agreement that says if the procedure is effective and you were in the non-treatment group that you should be able to get the real implant, free of charge, before any of the general public is eligible. It is not fair if you do all of this and then get no benefit at all.

Last, find out what happens in the research is moved to another site further away during the 19 months of the study or if a true cure comes along during that time.

It is a real pleasure to be writing about these steps toward a cure rather than coping skills.

Moving From an Asset to a Liability

The progression of PD is generally so slow that you cannot identify the exact moment you move to a new phase. Sometimes you can. The second week of April was when I moved from being an asset to a liability to both COPS and my family.

The story of what happened to me may be a good moral tale that could help you. I'm embarrassed to say, this is another case of you learning from my mistakes. Let me tell you what happened. Back in January I saw a neurologist for an annual checkup on my PD. I was having problems with my daily schedule of taking pills four times a day. On that schedule I took two forms of carbidopa/levodopa, Comtan®, and amantadine three times day with a different dose at bedtime. Because I was "wearing off" before my next dosage, the doctor upped my three-times-a-day to four-times-a-day plus the bedtime different set.

The doctor's assistant wrote out a schedule for my new medication regimen and gave me new prescriptions. I failed to notice that my daytime mix only included amantadine on only three of the four dosages. I might have noticed it when I picked up my pills from the pharmacy but I was preoccupied with how my new Medicare Part D drug coverage was working. Making it worse, my new drug program made it possible to get a three-month supply instead of my previous one-month. Further confusing everything was the pharmacy computer, accustomed to my one-month buying habit, did not stock the store for three months worth and I had to pick up the order in two parts The pill bottles for large numbers of pills were very large and were now broken into multiple bottles of the same drug.

So, I began the new regimen taking an amantadine with the first four daily pill sets instead of three. It wasn't until I started to run out of the amantadine that I discovered my error. The question was what I should do next. I knew the insurance company would not pay for a refill a month early. I couldn't buy any extra on my own without a prescription. Finally, I didn't want to call the doctor and say, "Look I'm an idiot. I took too many pills."

Males born in Iowa are not allowed to ask directions when lost or admit to doing something stupid. I had five or six pills left when I discovered my boo-boo so I thought I'll use them once a day to taper off amantadine altogether.

Amantadine, which I have been taking for over five years, was originally a flu medicine in use in Great Britain when a doctor noticed that, when prescribed to PD patients, it reduced some of their Parkinson's symptoms. I was taking it to reduce the dyskinesias that often accompanied my peak dose of carbidopa/levodopa. Dyskinesia is the writhing, involuntary movements that are best exemplified by Michael J. Fox. I hadn't been troubled by dyskinesias in a long time so dumping it, I thought, should be easy. At worst I could endure a little dyskinesias for a month until I could get more amantadine.

But, as we used to say back in Iowa, "My world went to hell in a hand basket." It took me forever to initiate movement and then it was very slow and I felt very weak. Entire days went by where I accomplished absolutely nothing. My wife was an Ohio-born female and therefore not bound by my percepts of Iowa manhood, entreated me to call the doctor but I insisted that amantadine had nothing to do with bradykinesia (difficulty in initiating movement, slowness).

After five days, forsaking my heritage, I called the doctor's office and in three hours I had a new prescription and in another three days I was back to, what I take to be, normal.

This little adventure put the newsletter in jeopardy. Last week was the week I should have devoted to putting the newsletter together. In fact, if you are reading this in an issue labeled May/June I am to blame for your missed newsletter. None of my personal jobs got done, not even reading my email. I'm sure the family thought that it might be time to look into assisted living.

This is how I went from being an asset to becoming a liability. Unless you are an Iowa-born male, if anything like this happens to you, call your doctor at once and confess. Don't put yourself and everyone else through hell just because you (like me) think you know how drugs work. A little knowledge is a dangerous thing.

If you are an Iowa-born male, call me and I'll give you the necessary passwords.

Communications

When I was growing up in Iowa in the 40's and 50's, we didn't have iPods, cell phones, instant messaging, personal data assistants, or lap top computers—thank God. I don't know if you have tried to talk to a teenager lately. I have, or to be more precise, I have tried.

iPods have caused an almost total breakdown in communications with the modern teenager. The ear buds, as they are called by Apple marketing, apparently burrow into the user's ear making them next to impossible to remove. Most teens have given up even trying. The iPod can hold over 10,000 tunes so they don't have to come up for air very often. At $.99 per tune, they have $10,000 in binary bits floating in the ether of their iPod (this is about three to four weeks of their future college expenses).

It seems to me that if you are the parent of a teen, you have one strike against you. If you are on the downhill side of 50, you'll soon be told you "don't understand young people today," and that is strike two. If you have PD, it's an automatic strike three.

In the best of circumstances, it becomes more difficult for us to communicate with people as our Parkinson's progresses. I'm eleven years post diagnosis, so I will speak from my experience. First, we loose volume in our speaking voice. It sounds like the normal volume to us because we are close by the source and have the advantage of additional support such as bone conduction of sound. Unless we speak, in what seems to us a shouting voice, we are not heard by waiters, cashiers, or teenagers.

Speaking in a loud voice reminds me of an Iowa story. A friend back in Iowa helped arrange a meeting with his intended's mother and his own mother. He told his mother that his intended's mother was very hard of hearing but was too vain to wear hearing aids. This would necessitate using a very loud voice to communicate with her and would explain her shouting back. Of course then he told the other mother the same thing. They shouted at each other for hours before they discovered the ruse.

But volume is not the only problem. I, along with the typical PD patient has what is called "mask" meaning that your face doesn't move enough to show emotion. This further impedes communication because people looking at you think that you are angry. Written communication is worse. Usually our hand writing is so small and jerky that even we can't read it. This is called micrographia by the doctors.

After your speech becomes soft and indistinct, you begin to slur your words. Then comes a general difficulty in putting together the words you really wanted. Your primary means of communication is a slurred jumble of words no one can hear. This is the hardest for me to accept. But I'm not finished with this topic.

One of the drugs I take to help control the symptoms of PD, works by making the neuron receptors more sensitive, thereby allowing me to get by with less dopamine. It has a side effect of also making the receptors that control my emotions more sensitive as well. I can't relate even a simple news story about something sad without my voice quaking.

The coup de grâce is that I am beginning to drool. Nothing says "old man" as loudly as does drooling. Drooling is a result of not swallowing as often as our body slows down. There is no warning; you just feel saliva running down your cheek or wake up to a wet pillow. While there are drugs that reduce saliva output, most patients do not like the "cotton mouth" feeling that results. You really have to be tough to endure PD.

While we are in this area of the body, we would be remiss not to discuss swallowing difficulties. I have those as well. Last year, I was evaluated by the otolaryngology department at the Ohio State University hospital. The test consisted of me eating different textured foods while they video taped me through an x-ray fluoroscope. They played back the tape for me and they pointed out how the epiglottis (the little flap at the top of the esophagus which prevents food from going into your lungs) was very slow to react. Choking or ingesting food into your lungs can be very dangerous.

There are techniques to reduce your risk (such as drinking water frequently during a meal to keep the pathway lubricated), but you should arrange a hand signal that your partner understands means you are choking and your partner should know the Heimlich maneuver. Incidentally, Dr. Heimlich is still alive, lives in Ohio, and has PD. Small world.

On your voice problems, there are many techniques you can employ. You should use your loud voice daily. If you don't have teenagers (nature's way of forcing you to use a loud voice), I recommend singing in the shower at full volume.

While in the shower make exaggerated facial expressions of each emotion to help your face move. Take a deep breath before beginning to speak.

There is much more to learn. Speech training provides a number of techniques and exercises to overcome some of the deficits I've noted.

I'll leave you with one more communication-problem story. Back when my daughters rode the same school bus (Riley was in fifth grade and Kaitie in second grade), Riley came home one afternoon and said that Kaitie had used the f-word on the bus.

I thought "Oh my goodness. What has the world come to that a second grader would use the f-word?" I thought the thing through and then took Kaitie aside and gave her a lecture on using bad words. She seemed to take it well. When I told her what the punishment would be for this transgression, she protested, "Dad, I don't think that fart is that bad a word."

When Golden Vocal Cords Turn to Lead

As Parkinson's progresses your voice becomes softer and more difficult to hear. The odd thing is, that to you, your voice sounds the same as ever. Apparently, the source of your voice is so close to your ear drums and is amplified by bone conduction; your perception of volume does not match anyone else's.

You'll first notice it when ordering a meal in a restaurant. The waiter, nowadays known as "I'll be the one helping you this evening", will not be able to hear your order. Finally your spouse will give up on you and tell the "one helping you" your order preceded by the dread "He will have the..." Referring to you in the third person makes you feel as if you weren't there or, like a small child, incapable of ordering yourself.

There are possible answers. The most generally employed is the Lee Silverman method. Courses in this technique are available from the Columbus Speech and Hearing Center and one regular class is specialized for Parkinson's and has been sponsored and paid for by COPS for many years. I've taken the course and can report that the main ideas are to put more effort into your speech and to practice speaking with volume.

I practice my voice exercises by singing in the shower as loud as I can. Unfortunately, this upsets the dog causing her to bark wildly. I don't know if it's my pitch or just my inability to carry a tune that bothers the dog so much. Deaf dogs would make the ideal pets but are hard to find. I seem to be able to find dogs with every other malady known to man or beast, resulting in my children's inheritance being drained off to the veterinarian. But I digress.

Last year, while meeting with an ear, nose and throat specialist, he suggested a procedure that I had not been aware of. His exam showed that my vocal cords were drooping which made them hard to produce sound with when they looked like noodles spilled on the kitchen floor. He suggested that he could inject the vocal cord with a substance that would raise and tighten them. I suppose the substance was not unlike that used by women interested in raising and enlarging a popular body part (or two).

The injection was through the front of my throat while I sat quivering. The procedure did work, but only for a couple of weeks. The therapist in the office asked why I did not try to shout. I explained that Iowans do not act crudely and shout at anyone. He said I should try and shout and he would give me a $100 if anyone ever thought that I was shouting. He has not had to pay.

So, I am back to singing in the shower. I do not know any opera, so the dog doesn't gain any cultural or any musical value at all for that matter. Surprisingly, there is no vet specialist in that area that will see my dog. Yet.

Advice from Experts

Iowans haven't always been the stoic, polite-to-a-fault people you see on the evening news every night filling sand bags trying to avoid being relocated to Louisiana. My generation of Iowans (those born in the late thirties and early forties) entered this world as heathen savages. It took all our parent's and grandparent's might to bend us into the ideal citizens one sees so often today.

I developed "lazy eye" about the time I started Kindergarten. The symptom was plain to see – one eye turned in. My mother took me to our family physician. I remember him dropping a pin into the carpet in his office and asking me to find it. I had one good eye so this was no problem for me. His conclusion was that, since my eyesight was good, I was just going through 'a stage.' Going through a stage at that point in Iowa history meant that they had no idea what was wrong but that whatever it was would probably correct itself in time.

This was an incorrect diagnosis. Proper treatment at the time would have probably saved my eyesight in that eye.

It will be hard for today's children to believe, but in 1946 I was the only child in Lincoln Elementary wearing eyeglasses. I was also the only kid whose right eye stared at his nose. I had to wait until 1952 to have it surgically straightened, which is only a cosmetic procedure.

When you have crossed eyes, people relate to you much differently. Iowans, when talking to each other, make eye contact. As the speaker with a crossed eye talks, the listener becomes confused about which eye to follow. People give up and take the easy way out by not looking at the other person but, rather, speaking to their shoes. How hard it is to relate to someone when they won't look you in the eye.

So, in Lincoln School, I was the only child with a crossed eye and the only one wearing glasses. Unlike a school today, absolutely no one then wore braces on their teeth, no matter how horrible a job nature had done. The idea was generally that you played the hand nature dealt you.

I, naturally, stood out. I was further disadvantaged; I could not play even mediocre baseball because having only one good eye limited my depth perception. They did not have safety glasses in those days, so most other sports were also out of the question.

Few of the boys at school would play with me, given my limited abilities. The girls only wanted to be near athletic heroes. When I appeared at a neighborhood softball game (where mothers were nearby to force my inclusion) and the captains would take turns choosing their teams. I was always the last selected and usually only with the agreement that my team be compensated for taking me by moving a strong player from the other team as proper compensation for this handicap. When they pitched to me, they rolled the ball on the ground. On the field I played a special position behind the pitcher, where I would not be hurt or interfere with the game. This did not impress the girls, but that's another story.

Worse than this was that everyone called me either "four eyes" or "cross eyed." Many times I went home in tears. The professionals at school told me I was too sensitive. These were only names, they said, and I should not let them bother me.

Flash forward now about twenty-five years. I'm still in Iowa and my marriage is in trouble. For the second time in my life, I sought the advice of a professional, this one claiming to be a marriage counselor. I was told that I was not sensitive enough. Go figure.

Well, boys and girls, what lessons do we learn from this story? First, we saw that doctors can misdiagnose. To be fair, physicians are much better today than they were sixty years ago. Still, it's you inside of your body and you are the final decision maker. Learn to be sensitive to what your body is telling you, at the same time ignoring the little voices in restaurants saying, "Mommy, look how that man is shaking." You have a right to question your doctor, understand your diagnosis and the reasoning behind this diagnosis. If your body tells you otherwise, maybe a second opinion is in order.

You have some responsibilities to your doctor as well. All of your different doctors should be told all of the drugs that have been prescribed for you, even those for other conditions. You should also tell them about any vitamin supplements or home remedies you are taking. Understand what each new prescription is for, when you should expect results, and when you should call the doctor back if things aren't working out.

Last, but every bit as important, look everyone in the eye when you speak to them. If you have PD, it may be hard to look into the eyes of another with PD who is a very advanced patient because of the fears it raises within us, but they are fellow humans and entitled to respect.

Do these things and I will make you an honorary Iowan. In addition to those requirements listed above, the only other responsibility will be occasional sand bag filling.

Meet Joe Btfsplk

If you are older than dirt and you used to read the daily comics, you may remember Joe Btfsplk. Joe was the guy in Lil' Abner with the rain cloud always overhead. Al Capp, the cartoonist, died in 1977, but I am the heir to that cloud.

It is altogether,fitting and proper, then, that I be the first to suffer from the problem I wrote about recently–the confusion that comes about because of the naming of the generic Sinemet. If you think I am making all of this up just to sell newsletters, I must warn you that I am collecting documentation as I go. I must also disclose that there is no charge for the newsletter, and thus, I have never been paid for any writing I have done.

The latest event occurred on April 10, when I noticed that my prescription for carbidopa/levodopa 25/100 SR was about gone, while I still had plenty of carbidopa/levodopa 25/100 left. I had picked up both prescriptions the same day, so they should have run out at the same time. Carefully checking the label, (as I should have done when I picked them up, had I been following my own advice), I found that the quantity dispensed was 225 and the instructions said "Take one half tablet by mouth five times a day."

Those were the count and instructions for the non-SR version, but the drug name out the outside of the bottle was correct and they were the correct pills. There were just not enough of them. I hastened henceforth to the pharmacy and spoke with the pharmacist on duty; after all, they owed me 225 pills. There followed a conversation that had a certain Abbot and Costello ring to it. She could not understand what the problem was. I told her to please show me the doctor's original prescription. I distinctly remember him writing "One tablet five times a day" and 450 for the quantity.

The pharmacist typed on the computer for many minutes, then opened the pill bottle I had armed myself with in anticipation of trouble. She took out several pills to compare them with the computer's image of what the pill should look like. Her jaw dropped, indicating she did not like what she was seeing.

She excused herself to find the prescription in question. She found that the prescriptions were refill orders that had been faxed in by the doctor. They were both for the non-SR form of the drug, and yet that prescription had been filled by the SR version and the SR name, but the dosing instructions and pill count were for the non-SR version. In other words, she was telling me that my doctor had sent the same prescription twice by error and they had filled one of them with a drug they did not have a prescription for.

The pharmacist complained about the similarity of names. I agreed and asked what she would recommend to simplify this whole mess. That is when she tried to correct me about naming by telling me that SR is "standard release" and CR is the longer-acting "controlled release." Apparently, she had mistaken me for somebody from rural Ohio and did not realize I was, in fact, a learned gentleman from Iowa who has been taking these medications since 1995. At last (I think in an effort to get me to lower my voice and vacate the premises), she told me she was only a temp pharmacist helping out in this store and asked me to return the next morning to speak to (yell at) the pharmacist in charge.

This I did. After discussions with the doctor's office, company executives, and the insurance company involved, they gave me the additional pills.

This leaves me still wondering how many times these prescriptions are screwed up and the doctor is seeing symptoms that are the result of the wrong prescription?

Since no one else will speak up and because I always seem to be the one with problems, I have a proposal. The formulation for the standard non-CR version of the drug should be changed to 26/104. I doubt this 4% will be noticed by anyone and it will provide some difference in naming.

If this fails, we should bring back another character from Lil' Abner – Fearless Fosdick. Fearless' most famous case was when a crook committed the perfect crime by putting poison in one can of beans in a supermarket and then committing suicide. To insure public safety, Fearless shot anybody attempting to buy canned beans. At least they found solutions in those days.

Shaving with a Straight Razor

Permit me, gentle reader, to recall a true story I heard back in the 1950s. A little two-year-old girl had contracted a blood disease and her blood type was very rare. Her four-year-old brother had the same rare blood type and it was determined that a blood transfusion from her brother would be the only thing that could save her. The parents and doctors went to the little boy and told him they wanted to take some of his blood to save his sister's life.

The little boy was wide-eyed and seemed scared, but he gulped and said yes. After the doctor had inserted the needle and the collection of blood began, the little boy asked, "How soon will I die?" He didn't know, and no one told him, that this was a harmless procedure on his part.

How many of the million-plus in this country with PD know much about it? The ratio of patients to support group members tells me that it is far too low. How many, like the little boy, are assuming the worst? When I attended my first support group meeting, I met several people who had lived with PD for nearly twenty years. They were still driving and could get around quite well, thank you. This information helped me relax and postpone further planning of my memorial service.

When my wife, Sandy, was pregnant with our daughter Riley, the OB, after performing one of the modern tests they do, asked us if we wanted to know the sex of the child still six months shy of being required to obtain a social security number. I said, "Of course," but Sandy wasn't sure she wanted to know, preferring surprise. This is apparently a typical split response from couples.

If there is information available, I want to know it–good or bad. This is because I grew up where people did such things as buy the "Farmer's Almanac" to get information on next year's weather before they decided what to plant. I remember one year it predicted a blizzard at the end of April/beginning of May. When it didn't appear, my folk went to church and thanked their maker for averting such a calamity. If we were the Central Iowa Parkinson Society, we'd have everyone writing in for our booklets with information on PD. On the other hand, it would be difficult to get people into support groups.

My grandfather, back in Iowa, had PD. Further, his PD began in the days before levodopa therapy was available. I remember as a little boy watching him trying to drink a cup of coffee in a restaurant. I have not seen tremor of that magnitude to this day. Coffee was flying in all directions. Iowa men in those days (and probably continuing to this day) do not permit women folk to feed them in public. When a lady at the next table looked at him with disapproval, he said, "Maude, it's the palsy and I can't do a thing about it." He referred to her by her name because everyone knew everyone else in Montrose, Iowa.

Grandpa Wardlow, who hated his PD, but didn't hide its symptoms and wasn't particularly embarrassed by them. I think that Iowans define embarrassment as something that could have been avoided but wasn't. Spilling a little coffee couldn't be avoided by Grandpa and wasn't an issue with anyone (save Maude). The rest of the country is now following Iowa's lead.

Grandpa Wardlow's major problem with PD was in shaving. Grandpa had always used a straight razor since his youth, carefully stropping on a horsehide and other material chained to the bathroom sink. The family feared that with his PD, he would cut his head off. Grandpa had seen the new safety razors that were on the market, but he, being a true Iowan, saw through the scheme immediately. You had to buy new blades from time to time. For someone using the same razor all of his life, this seemed the height of frivolity to continually spend additional money on shaving equipment.

Fortunately, Grandpa's job was being the warden in charge of the state penitentiary work farm. The farm was home to nearly a hundred inmates who grew food for the main penitentiary. The farm was self-contained to the point that it had its own barbershop tended to by Jake the barber. Jake was an expert with a straight razor and demonstrated his ability on a fellow he found in "flagrante delicto" with his wife after returning home early one day. Jake was convicted of double murder and given life in prison. He gave Grandpa a daily shave and that solved that. The take-away message here must be "look beyond usual means to solve PD problems."

Cascade Terrace

Back in my hometown in Iowa, most residents are working people and don't put on airs. A grocery store owner of my acquaintance, upon reaching retirement, sold the store he had built up over a lifetime. The sale left him with more money than he ever had during his working life.

In those days, if you had money and lived in Burlington, Iowa, you would aspire to live in a development called Cascade Terrace. This is where the doctors, lawyers, and others whose job description excluded heavy lifting, owned homes. Having ended a career of heavy lifting, his first purchase with his newfound wealth was a home in Cascade Terrace.

He was a bit disappointed to find his new neighbors stand-offish. Not a single new neighbor offered to help him unload furniture from the borrowed pickup that the previous neighbors had helped him load at the old house.

But shortly, he received a written invitation to join "The Cascade Terrace Men's Classical Music Appreciation Society." He said that he figured that the men in the new neighborhood were much more sophisticated than the old, and this was their way to get away from the wives on Sunday afternoon for a few beers, a card game, and a cigar.

He went to the next meeting, which was held in a member's house whose wife was out of town. To his surprise, the host began the meeting by putting a symphony on the turntable.

This seemed to be taking the ruse a bit far, he thought, but, when the symphony was over, the host announced that refreshments would be served in the other room. With a knowing smile, he repaired to the other room, only to find milk and cookies.

He said later of his experience, "You know, some of those devils went back for seconds!"

This is a true story. You can't make this stuff up. The reason I tell this story is that I want you to come to a PD support group meeting. I'll tell you what to expect so you will not be disappointed if no beer is served. First of all, I'll tell you what they are not. They are not "pity parties," where people sit around feeling sorry for themselves. They are not like an AA meeting, where you have to stand up and say things like, "Hi. My name is Michael and I have PD. My most intimate personal problems are..." I needn't go on here – you get the idea.

A support group is, first of all, a handful of very nice people. Many researchers have wondered why so many "nice people" seem to have PD. There have been papers written about the conjecture that only nice people get PD. If you look at those with PD, such as the Pope, Billy Graham, Muhammad Ali, and Michael Beetner, you will see the truth in this assertion.

(Someone is bound to write in, pointing out that historians believe that Hitler had PD. I say that is the exception that proves the rule.)

This group of nice people will probably include those at various stages of PD. They have learned some pretty ingenious coping skills and will share them. Often times, there will be a speaker talking about some aspect of PD. Because it will be a small group of twenty or so (it varies), you will be able to ask questions of your speaker.

Support groups for central and southeast Ohio are listed in every issue. There are special groups for early-onset PD who are still working, there are groups that meet in assisted care facilities, and there are groups for care partners, and so on. All groups welcome new members or those just wanting to visit. The contact person in the listing can tell you more about the group and give you exact directions to the location, if needed. If you want to start a new group, we will help you in many different ways.

(Insider's hint: I know of people who belong to more than one support group. We are fine with that.)

Check out a group and see for yourself what they are like. I expect the waiting lines when the cure becomes available will be long. This way you will know some of the others in line so you can have someone to talk to and to hold your place in line while you go to the restroom.

Fight Back

Last month brought more good news from the researchers working on PD. Several months ago, I wrote about the importance of "tools" when you are doing any job. We now have another tool to study PD. Researchers announced they have found a way to give PD to fruit flies. Fruit flies have long been a favorite of researchers because of their seven-day lifespan. Now scientists have both vertebrae and non-vertebrae models of PD.

According to what I read, the fruit fly brain has many similarities to our own. (This is probably knowledge I would have been happier not knowing.) The short lifespan allows scientists to quickly study the effect of a treatment over many generations. I do not know when a fruit fly is considered old (perhaps five days?)

The world being what it is today, I expect to be contacted shortly by a fly rights group concerned with the use of fruit flies in an inhuman manner. Given that they are inhuman, I will fight back against such a group that would have my brain further deteriorate rather than inflict the malady on an innocent insect. I am innocent as well. My PD is not (as far as we know) due to life style, or such.

I have grown quite attached to my brain over the years and cannot imagine life without it. Without it I would be condemned to a career in government service, undoubtedly in the taxation department. To be honest, however, the brain is my second favorite bodily organ.

An Example of Courage

How you fight back depends on your circumstance. Many with PD who are presently employed do not disclose to their employer that they have PD. They fear loss of their job, subsequent loss of health insurance, or being pushed off of their career track.

Our former treasurer here at COPS is in the real estate business. She did not make her PD common knowledge, fearing that some customers might be reluctant to ride in the car with her and such. Because the general public knows so little about PD, this is a legitimate concern.

This month, however, I received a letter Pat had mailed to her customers and friends. In the letter, she told about being inducted into the $10 million dollar club. This proves someone with PD can still do the job. Next, she revealed that she does have PD and that she is fighting it. In a brilliant piece of marketing, she then announced that she would make a donation to PD research at each closing from now on. That is how to fight.

An Opportunity for You to Fight

The Parkinson's Action Network (PAN) holds its an annual Public Policy Forum in Washington, D.C. The goal is to draw national attention to PD and have a direct impact on federal policy. You are welcome to attend. Not only will you hear from the top researchers about their progress, but you will also be making personal visits with our elected officials.

The more of us in the room, the greater the impact. Last time I attended, there were only about ten from Ohio registered. Ohio has an estimated 60,000 with PD. If, say, only 59,000 of us showed up in our senators' offices, we would certainly get their attention and probably their support.

To join us in this fight, contact the Parkinson's Action Network at 1025 Vermont Ave NW, Suite 1120, Washington, DC 20005.

Enlisting Others in Our Fight

The more who understand PD and the promise of a cure, the better chance we have of getting there sooner. Or, in fighting terms, the larger our army, the better our chances.

Something Else To Worry About

I learned something new about prescription drugs this past week that I thought I would share with you, dear reader. Permit me to provide a bit of background first.

It's a fortunate parkie who does not have something else going to hell in a hand basket, health-wise. You may remember me writing about my Grandfather Wardlow, who also had PD. He also had a lot of trouble with his prostate. I'll be interested to see when all of this gene research is finished whether or not enlarged prostates are linked to PD.

Anyway, I began recently to have problems with what the doctors call "urgency." This is when you really, really, have to go. The villain in this scenario is a prostate that has grown so large that it squeezes the little something that is ordinarily squeezed by a full bladder to signal its owner that it is time visit the facilities.

My urologist prescribed a drug that should help. After a few days, I called back to report that it didn't seem to be working. I was told to double the dosage. Again, that didn't work (and perhaps even seemed to make it a little worse), so I was advised to triple the dosage and that if that didn't work, to quadruple it, but to go no further.

Now the problem was definitely getting worse. My wife told me that it was obvious that his new medication was making things worse and that I should stop taking it. With some scientific condescension, I explained that the worsening condition was exactly what this drug was for. Perhaps the drug is not working for me, I explained, but it wouldn't cause the very symptoms it was designed to alleviate. I resisted her exhortations until the interval between my urgent dashes to the porcelain facilities were nearly five minutes apart. When I called the urologist's office this time, I was told to come down there immediately.

They told me that this drug can be a "paradox" drug, meaning that in some people it causes the very symptoms that it cures in others. I had always thought that a drug either didn't work or worked along some continuum from a little to a lot. I never considered the possibility of it turning 180° on me. Now I find that this happens on most all drugs, although Dr. Hubble tells me it doesn't happen often in routine PD drugs.

So now I will have different ground rules and expectations as I start any new drug. I was lucky. They told me that if I hadn't gone in when I did, I would have been in the emergency room that night for sure.

The moral is don't assume anything about a drug and, yes, listen to your wife more.

Another Drug Interaction Horror Story

A member of my support group experienced chest pain a few months ago and, appropriately, reported to the emergency room. It turned out to be acid reflux and the doctor prescribed Pepcid.

That solved the acid reflux problem, but his wife noticed that his PD had worsened. It got to the point where my friend completely froze up outside and had to be carried inside by his wife, who is, at best, half his weight. In total frustration, she asked herself what had changed. Pepcid is a widely used, over-the counter preparation and she told us that even the label claimed there were no drug interactions with it.

She stopped his taking Pepcid and he is slowly coming back. Coming back is very difficult when you miss as much exercise as he did. But he is a fighter and a loyal reader who has taken the advice in this newsletter and tried Tai Chi and had an exercise program.

The moral here is that we must always be careful and observant about the drugs we take, never make assumptions, and trust your wife.

The Demerol Problem Once Again

After the Pepcid story above, our support group heard of a woman going to the hospital for an out-patient procedure and having the staff try to give her Demerol even though she was taking Eldepryl (generic name segeline). Having read our exhortations against taking the contra-indicated Demerol, she said no, that there was a problem.

Her doctor (rather than the rational approach of checking the Physician's Desk Reference [PDR] book), he brought in another doctor to tell her that it was indeed no problem. To top it off, they brought a pharmacist up to confirm there was nothing to worry about. Much to her credit, she held her ground. One of our members upstate died after receiving this combination of drugs.

I make no excuses for doctors too smug to check a patient's warning in the PDR. They were acting like lawyers.

Many of the young doctors have little experience with drugs such as Eldepryl, which have disappeared from their original use, hanging on, only because of their use in PD. Demerol, on the other hand, is given freely at the hospitals like candy.

We have a booklet that tells you how to get through to those health care professionals who will do their best to give you Demerol. The booklet is actually a kit with adhesive labels to affix to your hospital chart, your bed, and an IV line. It's free for the asking, simply drop us a line. With it, you can live to give those doctors a copy of *The Girl Who Died Twice; Every Patient's Nightmare: The Libby Zion Case and the Hidden Hazards of Hospitals* by Natalie Robins.

Reading it will give them a few sleepless nights.

Parkinson's Doesn't Exist

Consumer Reports magazine gives an annual award known as the *Oyster Award* to companies with difficult-to-open packages. Manufacturers, in an effort to make products harder to steal in stores have made them impossible for those of us with PD or senior citizen status to open.

Regular readers know that I have railed on this subject before, but have no successes to my credit. Somehow, manufacturers feel that they bear no responsibility beyond theft prevention. Whether this is due to indifference or perversity is not known to me.

How can a product be called a "safety razor" when one or more fingers must be sacrificed to liberate it from its plastic packaging before productive use can be made? For those optimistic readers seeking their fortune by filling a clear public need by designing a product to open other products, I should warn you that the required hand-held nuclear device would probably melt the product along with the package.

I propose that COPS give an annual award to the people responsible for packaging so tough that not a single member can open it. I further propose that this award be packaged in impenetrable plastic.

You should be aware that you can have your pharmacy substitute the standard child/PD patient-proof tops for rather a non-locking version at no additional cost.

Perhaps, now that I think about it, it would not be all that much of a stretch to apply the Americans with Disabilities Act (ADA) to this problem. The ADA guarantees us access to public buildings and facilities – why not to products we need? A high-profile legal action against the manufacturers would force their admission that the products are un-openable. Of course, there would be wide-spread public support for our case. Alternatively, we could insist that the retailers be required to open the products during the checkout process, once their fear of shop lifters is moot.

While I am on a rant anyway, I would point to the Ohio senator who has refused to meet with PD delegations to his office in Washington, D.C., about an additional $100 million in PD research financing. He always sent a staffer to be his proxy and warn us that $100 million would imbalance the federal budget, with resultant dire consequences.

However, this same senator has not spoken out forcefully about sending 360 tons of $100 bills (12.6 *billion* dollars) into the Iraq war zone to be given away without accountability.

What am I missing here?

By the way, according to one site on the Internet, the cure is here. Or, more exactly, according to the site, neurologists have been in cahoots with drug manufacturers and Parkinson's doesn't exist. Moreover, auther says he can cure whatever it is in as little as five days. If this were not a newsletter, you could click here and go to his site. Until technology of newsletters catches up, to see this for your self, type in http://info.noelbatten.com/personal_treatment.html.

This man, Noel Batton, is not a doctor but a *Natural Therapist*, lives in Australia, and the secret of his treatment is having a chiropractor align your back. Then he teaches you how to maintain the alignment through proper relaxation and breathing. This is the bad side of the Internet. People from a different time zone or different hemisphere can cheat honest Parkinsonians out of their money, with no chance of his ever seeing a jail cell.

He quotes medical journals that he says support his contention that the Substantia Nigra plays no part in the disease. He has written a book (available only as a $29 download) called *Parkinson's–The Greatest Medical Blunder.* Remember that when they want to sell you something too good to be true, they are talking about this.

Trust me, I am not in the drug interest's pocket and I am not a neurologist, but I will pass it along when there is a cure. I do not expect to see neurologists suddenly go into joint practices with chiropractors and begin teaching breathing and relaxation techniques.

Any drug companies *wanting* to put me in their pocket should send a massive amount of money directly to me (small bills please).

Governmental Failure to Plan

I'm sure that many of you have been so involved in following Paris Hilton's problems that you may have missed the criticism of our government's failure to plan for the aftermath of the Iraq invasion and hurricane Katrina. I have discovered another case of inadequate planning that has been overlooked. This one is worse than Britney Spear's underwear planning. Allow me to elaborate.

In 1946 America's young men came home from World War II and quickly made up for lost time. This resulted in the "Baby Boom," which was noted by our government at the time. These "Boomers" went through life always the victims of inadequate planning, such as school facilities, even though their exact numbers were known at least five years before they even started school. Now this group is nearing retirement. Our government, therefore, has had almost 65 years to plan for their retirement and medical needs. Apparently, this was not sufficient.

The figures are startling. The number of Americans aged 65 and older will grow from 35 million in year 2000 to over 70 million in 2030. Those over 85 will grow from 4.2 million to 9.6 million in that same time period. These are *not* wild political guesses–these are people already born and aging uniformly (chronologically at least).

OK, what else has the government known since 1946?

First, studies have long shown that elderly people treated by doctors with geriatrics training do better than those treated without the benefit of such training. Second, this elderly population will require 36,000 geriatricians. In 2005 there were only 6,615 certified geriatrics specialists in the U.S. and the number has been going down rapidly.

Given these hard numbers, in dispute by no one, how did our government plan to overcome this problem? Answer: they didn't plan. How did this happen and why are we left holding the bag?

Many doctors see us as "less than desirable" patients. Due to low Medicare payments, geriatrics is probably the lowest paying of the medical specialties. Elderly patients often present at the physician's office with multiple symptoms from chronic or multiple underlying diseases. A younger person comes in with a single problem. Many times our problems cannot be cured, only some symptoms treated. This means we are less rewarding to doctors who would rather cure a patient, receive thanks, praise, and remuneration and move on. On top of all that, we take longer to deal with to make sure we understand our medication schedules and other therapies.

What is going to happen? Dr. Robert L. Kane, director of the University of Minnesota's Center on Aging, puts it this way, "Geriatrics is a lost cause. There are just too few [geriatricians] now and no sign that there is any growing interest among medical students."

What will be the result of inaction? Right now, Medicare patients account for a third of hospital patients and half of all hospital charges. Inadequate care, coupled with a burgeoning population reaching retirement and then having the ingratitude to live longer than ever before, will cost taxpayers added billions. Unfortunately, these taxpayers are our children.

Suggestions on dealing with the mess include increased use of nurse practitioners, I guess on the assumption that they will work for far less than doctors. Should Congress ever display an interest in this problem, they will probably deal with it as they have problems in the past–change the tax code. American business requires a tax break before they will do anything. I imagine there is a tax break for using the bathroom, which prevents our captains of industry from dying of constipation.

In fact, at the state level, a handful of states are increasing funding for geriatrics training. The federal government continues to ignore the problem, even though the scope of the problem is clear. Dr. Kane sums up by saying, "My guess is we'll push things to the precipice, panic, and then come up with a draconian solution and pump a lot of money into something that we could have solved much more cheaply years earlier."

Let me just add, "Welcome to old age."

Hey! Remember Us?

When stem cells came along, every news article on the subject mentioned how they could be used to defeat Parkinson's and Alzheimer's. It was estimated it would take five years to conquer PD with this new technology. The five years have come and gone several times now and I don't see anything near a cure on the horizon.

Recently, I read where stem cells had been used to create a pediatric heart muscle in the lab. The scientists who did the work said that the lab-grown muscle even twitched. They thought it would only be about three years until human trials began.

What were PD researchers doing during this period? I remember the effort to use pig stem cells to implant in PD brains. As everyone knows, there are more pigs in Iowa than people and Iowans would be willing to increase production to help. They did some human trials, but it didn't work out. Pigs are still used to provide heart valves for humans.

I was looking around the web recently for PD research. I wanted to see if anyone had looked into Pilates as a therapy for PD. I did find a study. (Well, at least that's what they called it.) Rather than a study that would have meaning in the world of PD research, this is what I found.

The study was not done double-blind as is required by, say, the FDA. In point of fact, the study did not even have a control group of any kind. The treatment group was exactly one person and he, at age 85, was not even a typical Pilates client. In other words, it was a complete waste of time. I can only hope that none of our money contributed for research funded this.

What do we do? We should insist on accountability and transparency in all forms of medical research. Why shouldn't the National Institutes of Health put all funded research on the web, followed by the final report by the researcher? Why don't we have a panel of researchers publish a list of the twenty most promising approaches for finding a cure? While I am not opposed to new and novel paths to find the cure, I think that we should get better organized.

We must insist on combining all of the different PD groups either into a single group or have all of the groups publish their results on the same web site. I would hope that papers, such as the one on Pilates described above, would prevent any further money being spent with the researchers and institution involved.

The PD Researcher's Press Kit

Today, I read my one thousandth press release about a possible cure for PD. Harvard University (otherwise known as the University of Iowa of the east coast), announced they had restored back to good health, mice with PD symptoms using stem cells As I read the end where it said that human trials where "five to ten years away," I realized I had read all this at least a thousand times before.

Besides being a critical Iowan, I am also a computer geek. After looking at several of these press releases, I have decoded the template used for PD research advances. The researcher merely inserts the information called for:

Press Release

For immediate release

Parkinson's Researchers Announce Major
Advance, Possible Cure for Parkinson's

<<date and city>> Researchers here
announced today that they have made a major
advance in the treatment of those afflicted with
Parkinson's disease that could lead to a cure.
Dr. <<your name>>, a researcher at
<<university or company>>, said, "We are very
pleased and excited by these results. We feel we

are now on the threshold of a cure for Parkinson's."

<<include here a sentence or two on what the study was about. (be vague)>>

Over one million Americans suffer from Parkinson's disease, including Michael J. Fox, Billy Graham, and Mohammed Ali. In Parkinson's disease, the brain does not produce enough of a substance that is required for proper movement, often producing rigidity and tremors.

"While we are excited by our results, we caution everyone that we are still in the very early stages of our resource and human trials are still five to ten years out," cautioned researchers. They went on to emphasize the need for substantial additional research and funding.

#30#

Hey, no thanks necessary.

My Deep Brain Surgery

I seem to have survived my first surgery and probably the second. What were they like? Well, dear reader, read on and I shall describe it as best I can. I must warn you, this is not for the squeamish or the faint of heart. Luckily, the brain has no nerve endings, so there is no pain from the probes that will be sticking into it. The reason I say lucky is because you must be awake for almost the entire procedure. This is because you must help guide the probe for proper placement.

First, who is eligible for Deep Brain Surgery? (DBS) Candidates must:

- have PD.

- be 75 or younger.

- not have other neurological conditions such as dementia.

- be in good enough health to be an acceptable surgery risk.

- not have had any prior neurological surgery.

- have tried all possible drug therapies without success.

- have reasonable expectations for the operation.

- be willing to accept the limitations of life with an implanted device.

- have insurance or the means to pay a really big hospital bill.

Your first stop will be to prove the above to the neurosurgeon. You'll probably begin with a neurologist examining you, confirming the diagnosis and producing a baseline of the various measures of the progress of your PD. Then you're off to a neuro-psychologist who will evaluate your short-term, mid-term and long-term memory. Your intelligence will also be measured so they can see if the operation diminishes your intellect. You'll be told a complex story and then quizzed about it later in the interview. You'll be asked to name every fruit you can think of. Then you will be asked about naming vegetables. This will be followed by asking you to name every non-proper noun you can think of beginning with the letter "N" and then "P." As I was listing "N" words, the neuro-psyc told me to switch to "P" words. My first two "P" words after the flood of 'N" words were pneumonia and pneumatic. She smiled and I knew I had passed.

Why all of these restrictions? You will remember the last time neurosurgeons thought they had the answer to life's problems—the lobotomy. They don't want to make that mistake again.

My first surgery was scheduled for the 29th of August at the Cleveland Clinic. I'm going to be very frank about the whole thing and I am trusting that no one from the Clinic will be holding my brains in their hands as they read this. Cleveland Clinic has apparently resisted using computers until recently. My file has been lost numerous times, somewhere between neurology and neurosurgery, causing delays. The staff can be insensitive to a patient's time line. The patient has made the commitment to proceed with surgery and the staff will say something like, "Neurosurgery will call you to schedule surgery. If you don't hear from them within six weeks, call them back." Their urgency is different than yours.

The past computer aversion leads each doctor or other nurse/practioner you meet to ask the same questions.

What drugs do you take and when?

What surgeries have you had in the past?

Are you allergic to anything?

What illnesses have you had or presently have?

The solution is to arrive with many photocopies of the answers to each of these questions.

Beginning March, I was first examined by Dr. Giroux (neurologist) and Dr. Rezai (neurosurgeon). It was July before I was scheduled for the end of August.

The Clinic asked me to appear at 11 a.m. the day before for MRI's and admission to the hospital. They take a lot of pictures of slices through the brain. You are always told to lie still in an MRI, but this time they mean *really* still. I had to have two sets repeated because I swallowed in one set and moved my jaw in the other.

Then it was up to hospital admissions to get checked in. Admitting had handled all of the pre-admission work over the phone, so they took a copy of my insurance cards (a ritual that all hospitals observe) and told me to be seated while they found me a bed. Beds are in short supply at the Cleveland Clinic. It took an hour and a half before they finally found a spot for me on the urology floor. I'm not proud–neurology, urology, whatever. The nurses may be more used to dealing with the other end, but all they had to do for me was keep me alive and not let me eat or drink after midnight. Because there is a nursing shortage there (and at every other hospital in the solar system), the nurse said she would set up the plumbing for the IV at her shift end (7 p.m.) and then a practical nurse could actually start the IV at 12 p.m.

Every time someone draws blood from me they always compliment the way my veins stick out. I do not like unsightly veins, but I hate needles more. I've never had trouble with an IV or drawing blood.

The nurse stuck in the first needle and didn't hit the vein. She wiggled the needle around and back and forth, just as they must do in terrorist questioning. She finally gave up and abandoned that site for another. IV kits come with two needles to allow for this. The second one hit after the same amount of tugging and jiggling.

At midnight the nurse's aide came by to start the IV and take my drinking water. This IV hurt more than any I'd ever had before. IV's are monitored by a machine that sets off an alarm if the IV is not dripping properly. Shortly after insertion, my alarm went off. I called the nurse and they jiggled the needle until the machine alarm stopped beeping, indicating the flow was correct.

The pain continued until I finally said to myself, "This isn't right." I summoned the nurse and she lifted my now very swollen left arm and said, "The IV slipped out of the vein. We'll have to re-do it." She got another kit and made two futile attempts on my right arm. She said, "I give up." Another nurse came in with another kit and had the same results. When the third nurse came in, I inquired as to her skills in IV placement. She claimed that she never took more than one stick and my case did not dispute her claim or break her record. Still, I had two very sore arms.

At 6 a.m. two doctors appeared at bedside and said they were there to prepare me for surgery. They unwrapped two sterile trays. One tray was used to cut my hair off and the other contained the sterile pieces of the halo. The halo is used to lower the probes into the brain. It also serves as a reference point for the MRI pictures that were taken previously.

Now, a metal halo cannot be used with an MRI so, before surgery began, I was given a CAT scan, which uses X-ray instead of magnetism. The CAT scan can be matched to the correct points in the MRI. This reference point is very important when you must be with 1 mm of the correct spot in your brain. In the real world, this means everything must be very tight so nothing can slip. Four pointed screws affix the halo to your head. Your head is swabbed with orange antiseptic and the screw sites where your skin will be punctured are numbed with a local anesthesia. The screws tightened just short of your brains coming out your ears. This is the lower half. The upper half awaits downstairs. The upper half is used as the guide for the probes they put down into your brain. This is what I looked like after the lower half was placed.

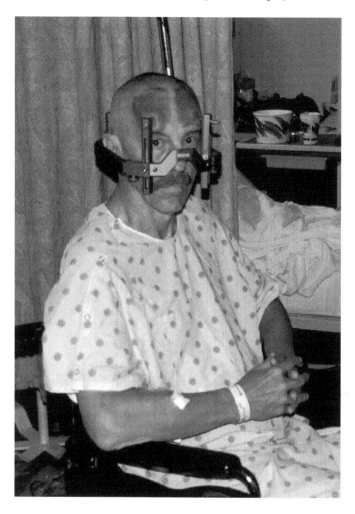

The CAT scan was only four minutes. On the way to the operating room, the doctors asked me which side they should do first. They explained the advantages of each side and they suggested the left brain first because that controlled the right side of my body, which was the dominate side.

During this discussion, I was wheeled through a maze of operating suites (they have 61 in total) and I could look through the doors as doctors, with sharp objects in their hands, bent over bodies, plying their trade. My operating room was quite large because, being a teaching hospital, there were several students in attendance. Everyone was upbeat and helpful. There were two anesthesiologists, a young nurse whose main job was to see to my comfort, a neurologist who would help with finding the correct spot, and Dr. Rezai, the neurosurgeon.

The hospital had called me several weeks prior to ask if I would mind if a Japanese television crew recorded my operation. I gave my permission, but they never showed. There went my chance for Japanese stardom.

Because of the halo that restricts your vision, people must bend down and sort of shout in your face. The room has a CD player and patients are invited to bring a favorite CD to play when the doctors are not listening to your brain. I had chosen Mozart. One of the doctors who had been conferring with the scans came over and marked my scalp with a felt-tipped marker where the incision was to be. Because I was so fascinated by the marks on my head, I did not see the anesthesiologist putting something in my IV.

I awoke with a start sometime later to find that the scalp cutting and the drilling of two holes were done. Mozart had been replaced by white noise (the kind of hissing noise one hears when selecting a TV station that is not on the air). When the noise got louder, they knew we were in the target zone. Dr. Cooper kept me busy by asking questions such as "Can you name the days of the week?" and "Can you count backwards from 100 by threes?" He would then take my arms and move them back and forth as quickly as he could. We could hear a swishing sound in the white noise.

By flexing my forearm, wrist, and so forth, we found the spot where they all swished. Now we played "How many fingers am I holding up?", "Follow my finger with your eyes," "Smile," and "Show me your teeth." Once we were at the spot, he did a normal neurologist's check of strength by hand squeezing, leg lifts against pressure and foot flexing. He tested my ability to extend my arms and then touch my nose with my finger tip.

Everyone was very serious at this point and watching closely for anything out of the ordinary. This would not be a good point to explain Atomic Mole People and their plan to turn all humans into living toilets. In fact, my earlier questions about the availability of a non-smoking surgery suite and my asking Dr. Rezai if he had washed his hands first, were met with serious answers about hospital policies.

Back to the operation, once satisfied they were in the correct spot, they replaced the probe with the actual lead. That being done they did a series of tests to see where the baseline voltages were, probably to give the programmers a starting point. They do this mainly by watching the back of your tongue as they increase the voltage. This must be the first part of your body to respond. At one point in this process, I could feel my stiffness relax completely. Hallelujah.

I was fairly comfortable during the operation, given that my head was bolted to the table, restricting my movement. I had a dry mouth due to lack of hydration, so the nurse would swab my mouth with a damp swab or give me a very small ice

chip from time to time. I also received two doses of Tylenol
to control pain. This was provided in liquid form by the
anesthesiologist–probably union rules.

Surgery began about 7:25 and it was about 2:30 when we
finished. I complimented the staff on being so quick. For
most patients, the whole thing takes much longer. Dr.
Cooper allowed as how those words had never before been
spoken in this operating room, but that he was looking
forward to seeing the early evening news that night for a
change.

The nurse or one of the doctors left the OR about once an
hour to tell my wife and daughter in the waiting room what
was happening,– a nice touch.

The recovery room was pure chaos. One poor resident was
earning his stripes by tending to a large number of patients at
the same time with, a limited nursing staff. There was not a
bay open for me,, so I got a spot in a hall way that is used for
overflow. Visitors are not allowed in recovery, other than one
short visit after the patient is awake. The visitor must be
invited and escorted. My wife was not given a chance to come
in for some time because more acute cases were dealt with
first. I finally got a CAT scan appointment for 6:30. I was to
get another CAT scan to be certain there was no bleeding on
the brain. That finally accomplished, I was released from
recovery. There were no beds available anywhere in the
hospital, so I had to remain in recovery all night. There are no
TVs in recovery or anything else to distract you from your
pain. People do not speak in hushed voices and fellow
patients groan and scream as they see fit. It was a very long

night. By morning, the operating rooms began to fill and they had to find someplace to get me out of the way. Finally, an exit hallway, outside of children's intensive care unit, was found open and I was taken there. Besides the pain of the surgery, the catheter that was inserted while I was in the OR was leaking and making the bed wet. I was uncomfortable and wanted to go home. The doctors released me about 3:30 and we were back home by six. This is how I looked the next day.

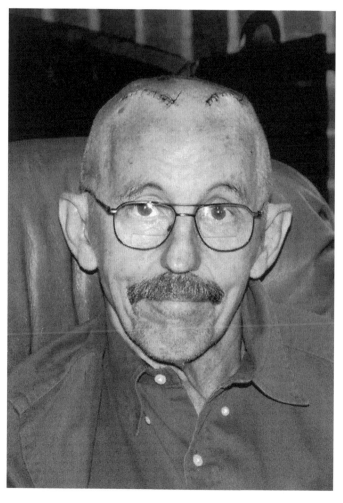

On September 11th I returned to have the whole thing put together. The wires from my brain had been left in a coil on the top of my head. This second operation was to run the wires down my scalp, behind the ears, and connect to the batteries implanted on both sides of my collar bones. This operation was the more traditional general anesthesia operation. Two more scalp incisions and two chest incisions and I was finished. The final event was an X-ray to confirm everything was hooked up. Cleveland clinic still did not have any rooms other than my hallway in children's intensive care and I went there only briefly to change into street clothes.

Overall, the doctors were excellent. The nurses were in short supply, but there were more available at Cleveland Clinic than the Columbus hospitals. As fast as modern hospitals spit out patients, they still have a room shortage. They are building everywhere in that complex, so there must be additional rooms on the way. I don't think you can bring your own room.

DBS Adjustments

In my continuing quest to be able to dance at my daughters' weddings, I have been writing about the deep brain stimulation (DBS) treatment I am undergoing. Last month I wrote of the operation, which probably sounded grimmer than it was. A few people wrote to me, praising my bravery in undergoing the surgery. This is flattering but untrue. In early October, the Cleveland Clinic celebrated their 1,000th patient for DBS. In other words, in northern Ohio, there at least are a thousand people braver than I.

 The news lately has had several stories about DBS, but not for Parkinson's. The TV program *Dateline* interviewed my neurosurgeon about the work that he had done on patients with intractable depression. The wires were implanted in another part of the brain and two patients treated were able to resume a normal life. Very recently, a case was reported of a man with a brain injury that left him paralyzed and virtually mute. A stimulator was placed in the thalamus above where they place it for PD. After surgery, he could move his left side and communicate using coherent words.

Of course, immediately the ethicists argued that, this being the case pre-op, how did they get his informed consent to surgery? There is a can of worms for you.

But I digress. After waiting two weeks after my second surgery, it was time to turn on the devices and begin the programming process. By "programming," they mean setting a number of different parameters in the stimulators to maximize their effectiveness. For example, they can set different voltage levels, different signals, polarity, and different areas of the probes to use. This is accomplished by putting a small device over each stimulator and using a tiny LCD screen and stylus to select parameters from a menu. Parkinson's is different for everyone, so they use this process to find the optimal balance of stimulation and drugs to maximize your quality of life.

The first session, you come in without your daily dosage of PD medicines. They then set your device to a starting voltage, have you take your normal dosage of drugs, and observe the improvement. In my case, I could move faster than before, my arm-swing returned, and my muscles were not nearly as tight as before. Before dismissing me for the day, they asked to sit in the waiting area for a half-hour so they could check and see if I was going to be OK with this setting.

They were running a little late. After about 40 minutes in the waiting room, all hell broke loose. My arms and legs began to dance about to the point where I looked like Michael J. Fox on crack. I could not hold my head up or maintain any significant posture. My wide-eyed wife called for help. Upon seeing me I was whisked back in and reduced the voltage to 1.5. The dyskinesias stopped. A good sign, they said, indicating a brain that had high sensitivity to stimulation. Home I went, with this low voltage to acclimate my brain to stimulation. My walking was worse because my new release from stiffness meant that the same energy put into walking yielded a much longer stride, which my already beleaguered balance system could not handle. I was restricted to a walker at all times.

While back in Columbus, I began a rehab program, concentrating on improving my gait (apparently required before I can begin dance lessons). There is a special rehab facility in Columbus specializing in neurological rehab. They are very good.

By the way, when I was up in Cleveland at the doctor's office, who did I meet in the waiting room but Dave Purdy. Dave is a few weeks ahead of me post-op and has just about completed his programming. As we compared notes, he demonstrated how well he was doing by getting up from his wheelchair and running (and I do mean running) around the waiting room. Had his doctor been witness to this display of ambulatory dexterity, she would have gone into immediate cardiac arrest.

My progress to-date is increased mobility and larger handwriting. I never experienced much tremor, so that wasn't an issue with me. Others have commented about my increased facial expression. That's the good news. The bad news is apparently something went horribly awry during my surgery, which has caused my hair to re-grow all gray.

Another bit of good news is that none of the various theft detectors I have been through have turned off my stimulators as the manufacturer warned. I have not yet traveled by air to find out if the authorities are going to assume I had small bombs implanted instead of stimulators.

Hacking

Back in the 1950s, I read a story in *Popular Mechanics* magazine about a new device they called an "electric brain." They said that this device could do the work of a hundred mathematicians and never make a mistake or take a break. Back then, computers, as they were also called, were very expensive. The first IBM computer, the IBM 650, used vacuum tubes and enough of them to heat a six-room house. This made them so expensive that IBM marketing experts predicted that it would likely be that only three or four computers would ever be sold. It seemed that only the federal government, AT&T, GM, and maybe a university or two would be able to afford a computer. (They ended up selling more than 2,000 of this model, thereby launching the computer generation.)

Still in high school, I decided I wanted to build computers. The University of Iowa had a computer and even offered a course on how to program it. So, beginning in January of 1960, I took "Programming Digital Computers," which was the only course offered on computers.

It turned out that the best in each class was offered a job at the University as a programmer. I was in heaven. The computer was the IBM 650. I remained in computers the rest of my professional life. Back then, I knew just about everything there was to know about computers and technology.

Bob and Ray had a character they used called Biff Burns. Biff was a baseball coach who had been coaching a little too long. Once he said, "I dunno. This game passed me by some time ago." That is how I feel today. I rely on teenage daughters to program my cell phone, alarm clock, digital camera, address book, slide screen and God only knows what else is in there. I own an iPod and don't know how to turn it on.

Yesterday, I read that Medtronic announced that computer hackers could hack into an implanted pacemaker and re-program them. They only mentioned the heart pacemaker, but I assume they can also hack into my deep brain stimulators. This would allow some teenager to seize control of my DBS and turn me into a wildly dyskinetic puppet.

Well, great What do I need? A firewall implanted? A password required to be entered every morning?

Medtronic was already reeling from a problem of leads coming loose with heart defibrillators and now, this hacking thing. This must have made trial lawyers' hearts beat a little faster even without a pacemaker of their own. Last week, however, the Supreme Court offered up a decision that was little noticed outside of court rooms, houses of ill repute, and other places infested by lawyers. The court held that manufacturers of implantable devices cannot be sued for any problems with their devices.

The legal theory is that the Food and Drug Administration is responsible for assessing the risk involved with an implant and if they find the risk acceptable for the potential good they do, no one can sue if problems occur. Otherwise, the court reasoned, the law suits may cause products that aid many others to be withdrawn from the market. I only wish I had a bit more confidence in the FDA's ability to make good decisions. It will be tough. Will they accept a 3% death rate, or 10%, or, like in a complete democracy, a majority rules We are talking about the federal government, so it could be even be, like the senate, where it takes 61% to prevail.

At least we are only talking about devices that could damage our brain or heart. If we restrict sales to Tea Party candidates, no one will notice.

Smile, Smile, Smile

PD has, I think, more symptoms than Donald Trump has vanities. Many PD symptoms do not seem to be major problems, such as falling, but one is more important than it is given credit for. One such symptom is called "mask" by doctors. It is the expressionless face that is typical of PD patients.

Now, why is that important? Thank you for asking. Many of you think that you are well evolved from the caveman. Not so. For example, we shake hands. What we are really doing is showing the new person that we do not have a weapon in our right hand. At the same time, we smile to show that we are friendly. Absent that smile, it looks as if we may change our mind about hurting them.

We smile at strangers with whom we make eye contact and if they do not respond with a smile, we worry. When someone helps us, we usually say thanks, but thanks without a smile is taken by the helper as a sign you are displeased with them or grouchy. Unless we are Donald Trump and carry a mirror with us at all times, we are not aware that the smile we thought had gone out was intercepted by some missing neurons in the brain.

It's the same as speaking. You have to put a conscience effort into each smile. For me, that means parting my lips and mugging a big smile, which comes out as a regular smile. If you don't put the effort into it, people will ignore you. In fact, the smile is more important than the thank you (my mother might disagree).

Some faces, and mine is one, are such that they look extra scary absent a smile. Donald Trump looks goofy with or without a smile (his mother may disagree or not). The Navaho Indians believe that a baby is not a person until they smile. Having PD should not mean you give up your personage.

Falling With Riley

I have a daughter who officially became a teenager this July. The other day, we were talking as we walked down the hallway at home on our way to the computer in my den. It is well known that I lack the physical graces. What is somewhat less known is that I also lack whatever graces are associated with an orderly office or work environment. This latter grace problem had been detected by my wife, who insisted, when we built our house, not only that the door to my den be paneled by obscuring glass, but that the door be divided so that only half would normally open, thus always hiding at least 50% of the view.

Like most teenagers, Riley is growing like a weed more than either of us fully appreciates. So it was that, as we walked through the half-door, our hips collided and we bounced back from the door. This happened in every Three Stooges movie I ever saw. Just like Moe, I immediately tried again to be first through the door. Riley, seeing me trying to make light of the situation, also tried to be first. Youth will win out in these situations. The only problem was I was thrown off balance.

When a parkie gets even modestly out of balance, we find that the slowness of our movements (medical term bradykinesia), will cause us to fall before we can move to regain balance. I fell.

Falling is a little extra scary for a parkie. The reason for this is that we know sooner that we are going down and so there is more time to anticipate and fear the outcome. If we have fallen before, we realize that our bradykinesia will also limit the normal human defenses of moving the arms to protect ourselves and cushion the fall. Falls can be serious business, especially if you are alone. If you have loved ones nearby, you scare the dickens out of them.

I was not hurt, but Riley was left with new fears for my safety and a feeling of guilt. I was left wondering if, when she as a teenager goes through the normal feeling that her parents are a disgrace to society in general, I will be thought of as a double embarrassment?

Already I have heard, with my own ears, classmates ask if I am her grandfather. To be fair, we can't blame Parkinson's for everything. I am old enough to be her grandfather. After all, she has a sister who is 34. In grade school, when she told about her family and the age of her brother and sister, the teachers often thought she was lying because that would make her siblings older than the teachers themselves.

It gets worse. My youngest daughter Kaitie, who is 10, has had the experience of me falling in her classroom in front of the entire class. My cane got tangled up in the damn little chairs they have, throwing me off balance and into a swan dive onto their desks. The side benefit to this lack of the physical grace is that, whenever the class sees me coming, everything stops. The kids make a path for me while the teacher frantically searches out an adult chair to seat me before I can fall again. It's as though they saw Godzilla coning down their hallway

An official at the National Institutes of Health was asked at a hearing what it would take to cure Parkinson's. He replied that it could be cured, given $1 billion and five years.

Did Congress recognize this as a bargain and tell them to get started? Nope. A billion dollars is a lot of money for most of us but not a lot in a trillion dollar economy. Where would the money come from? I would suggest that we first close the loop hole that unpatriotic corporate executives are using to "move" corporate headquarters to a post office box in Bermuda to avoid U.S. taxes. The Navy spends billions for nuclear submarines to poise off the Russian coast to flatten them if need be. We don't do that to any other NATO member.

Call or write Washington now. Tell them we can't wait forever. I'm writing to tell them in terms that they will understand. I am an old man who will soon have two teenage daughters in the house. I feel guilty that I cannot be more "normal" for the last two children. I also worry that I have given them some gene that predisposes them to Parkinson's or that I am also probably exposing them (unwittingly) to some substance or chemical in their environment that will trigger the disease. This is why I am mad at Congress

The Downside of Falling

The previous piece was written some time ago and I have had numerous falls since. It is no longer funny. Although I do remember Robert Benchley visiting Dorothy Parker in the hospital after one of her numerous suicide attempts. He told her, "Dorothy, you've got to stop this. You're liable to get hurt." Benchley aside, falling is a very serious problem for those with PD.

In the wider world of older people, one dies from a fall every 29 minutes in this country. Every 15 seconds a senior fall results in a trip to the emergency room. This latter group ends up with broken bones, including hips, which take a long time to heal, or cuts and bruises and such.

We all want to maintain a degree of mobility, but falls are probably the main villain. Physicians are the people who may be the most concerned because they have seen what falls can do. And the damage we can do to ourselves is getting greater as time goes by because of the electronics we have just under our skins, such as deep brain stimulators, heart pace makers, and such, along with the results of delicate surgeries that can be destroyed in a single fall.

PD patients are especially vulnerable because we have only age to contend with but also our Parkinson's, which gives us new balance problems, tremor, and bradykinesia (slow movements that do not allow us to get our hands out to either catch ourselves or protect ourselves in a fall). Joints and restricted movement are also a problem.

If all this wasn't enough, many of the drugs prescribed for our PD make the situation even worse. Wait, there's more. Patients often present to a doctor with more than a single ailment. In medical school, students are taught the rule, "patients may have as many diseases and problems as they damn well please." Neurologists I have met have never treated a case like mine where there is PD and a spinal cord injury. This later fact puts one too many variables in the equation. To be safe, they will prescribe a walker or some other device to keep you from falling.

I have found a better answer (at least in my case) is to slow down and think about what you are doing. If you're like me, you are used to hurrying in the style that today's society expects. If you are like me and are retired with no further need to hurry, you can learn to slow down and appreciate life more while also avoiding the trip to the ER.

Thinking Outside the Box

Some years back there was a brain teaser that had nine dots in a box. The goal was to connect the dots with three straight connected lines. Most people were unable to solve the problem because they tried to draw their lines within the box, even though that was not a stated requirement. I believe this is where the term "thinking outside the box" came from.

I'm guilty of not thinking outside the box quite often. A perfect example is last month's announcement of new research. Here is what I knew:

1) Dopamine is used in the lower body to regulate the heart.

2) Dopamine cannot pass through the blood/brain barrier.

Given these facts, I should have asked myself, "Where is lower body dopamine made?" My box was drawn around the brain and its dopamine-producing problems.

Someone (obviously intellectually superior to me) asked that question and it turned out that the retina of the eye contains those cells. In an experiment using six human subjects, it was shown that it is possible to implant those cells into the brain and achieve positive results. Now we have yet another route to a possible cure.

One of the men I met who influenced my life was Dr. William Shanner. Dr. Shanner was an educational researcher in California when our lives crossed. Bill (something I never called him when he was still alive) was also an inventor. He invented things when he saw a need. Once, in the early days of airline travel, he watched a stewardess distributing meals on a flight. (Those of us with gray hair remember when airlines made an effort greater than today's 0.75 oz. of miniature pretzels.)

The flight was rough and the poor woman kept having the dishes and coffee cups slip off the plastic trays they were using. That led him to invent a paper tray liner with a high friction surface that was quickly adopted by all the airlines to solve the problem.

He traveled a lot and noticed that he was not alone in being confused about what time it was back home. People would add two hours when they should subtract two, and so forth. He patented a watch with two hour hands. As he put it, "One is for where your body is and one for where your heart is." Bill was not without a sense of marketing.

He ran a small engineering company near Monterey, California, as a side venture. The Union Pacific Railroad came to his firm with a problem.

They were shipping cantaloupe from the Monterey area to Chicago and points east by rail. They had to ice the cars down to preserve the melons. It took tons of ice and replacing the ice along the way was a pain. They asked him to design a mechanical refrigeration unit for their boxcars.

I guarantee that 99.99% of engineering firms given this customer request would have produced a refrigeration unit. Not Bill.

He saw the real problem as how to get cantaloupe to Chicago as cheaply as possible. To find the answer, he studied cantaloupe. Cantaloupe, he found, ripen from the inside to the outside, unlike most fruit. He then identified the substance that the vine sent to the melon to tell it to begin to ripen. He synthesized this substance and patented it.

The solution he returned to the railroad was to pick the melons green and hard, inject them with his patented "start to ripen now" substance, and ship them in regular boxcars. They would be ripe shortly after arrival in Chicago. Rather than making a few thousand dollars for a one-time refrigeration unit design, he made money on every melon they shipped from then on.

I encourage all of you, and especially Parkinson's researchers, to think outside the box.

This is where the best answers to a problem can come from. In the case of the nine dots, it's the only place an answer comes from. Ask yourself what the real problem is. The problem in my last example was not how to build a boxcar refrigeration unit. It was how to get cantaloupes to Chicago as cheaply as possible. Review every premise. Some of what you learned in school is no longer true. Are your assumptions correct? Is there another approach? Last, don't overlook the obvious, but don't trust it implicitly either.

An Extremely Modest Example

I put up four hooks in our closet at home so we could hang our pajamas and such. I figured four hooks (two each for the Mrs. and me) would be enough. Before long, as you might guess, I did not have room to hang my PJs. Pleading my case for one hook would yield space temporarily until she forgot about it.

Thinking about the handling of disabled parking, I came up with the solution shown below.

It worked for about six weeks, a success in my book.

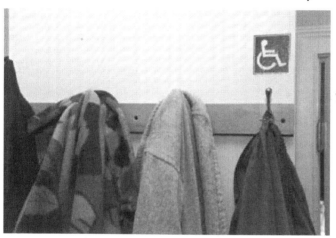

One Last Rant

I love the English language. It is constantly growing, adding new words at an astonishing pace with no approval needed by a controlling agency (unlike the French). In the past few months, we have added "twitter," "tweeting," and "sexting." Sometimes, it is even necessary to go back and update a word. Linguists call these words "retronyms."

A good example is the word "guitar." Guitar served us well for many years, but when someone invented the electric guitar, we needed a better word to describe the original guitar. The retronym for guitar is "acoustic guitar."

A study of 482 hospitals and health care facilities found nearly 200,000 medication errors in 2002. More than 3,000 of these resulted in patient injury. You and I take a lot of prescribed drugs every year. We should be concerned about these errors. I first experienced the problem first-hand in a hospital. Upon admission, I was asked what drugs I was taking, their strength, and frequency. I provided the information, using the generic name for those generic drugs I took, and the brand names for the rest. In two different hospitals, there was confusion in their pharmacy. The Cleveland Clinic repeatedly sent incorrect drugs, frustrating both me and my wife. Even after a pharmacist came to my bedside to straighten out the problem, he left confused and only diminished the problems.

The problem revolved around Sinemet®, long the gold standard for treating Parkinson's symptoms. The generic equivalent is carbidopa/leveodopa, which I take. When this drug first came out, it was in only tablet form. Sometime later Sinemet® CR was released, the CR standing for "controlled release," which meant it released the drug over a prolonged time to smooth out the peaks and valleys. Apparently, no one thought about guitar naming and the previous version did not receive a retronym.

Matters got worse when generics appeared the scene. Some manufacturers called their controlled release version "ER," meaning extended release. Another manufacturer called their version "SR" for sustained release. Still, the initial version did not get a name change. To be fair, every unique drug is given an 11-digit number by the Food and Drug Administration (FDA). I know of no one who uses or even knows the numbers of the drugs they take.

To make matters even worse, I take both forms of carbidopa/levodopa at the same 25/100 strength five times a day. I am always getting the wrong one. The insurance company handling my Part D Medicare coverage says they know how important it is to get my prescriptions correct. To avoid getting the wrong drug, they send me a wallet card listing my prescriptions for emergencies and visits to my doctor and pharmacist. A copy of my card is shown below. Notice that they, too, are confused about my first two drugs. By the way, Humana, even with 3.5 million people depending on them for drug coverage, provides inadequate information.

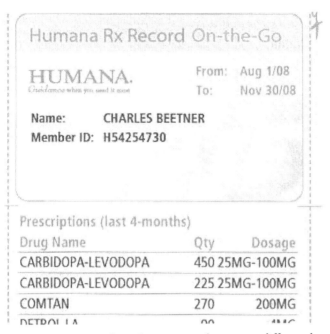

Notice that the two top entries have the same name but are two different drugs. Even Humana can't get it right.

Sometimes I hear people call the original form of the drug "immediate release." This is a good try, but what would you call the form of carbidopa/levodopa that one puts under the tongue to make it dissolve faster than any other form? It is marketed as a "rescue" drug because it is the fastest way to get it in your blood stream if you freeze.

Each generic manufacturer uses a different shape and color for their pills and your pharmacy can switch manufacturers whenever they can get a better price. This also makes it hard for us to know whether we have the correct medicine after it is in our hands. I've always been told that you should not break a CR pill in two because it then releases too soon. I wonder why some manufacturers score their extended release pills to make them easier to break in two. This takes away yet another clue from us.

What are we to do when we are given a drug inadequately labeled and in an unfamiliar pill form? What can be done to clear up this confusion? Medical errors are a leading cause of death in the U.S., killing between 44,000 and 98,000 Americans each year, according to various studies. Anesthesiologists, twenty years ago, had a patient death rate of one for every 5,000 cases. Some said this merely showed that surgery was risky and patients are more litigious.

In 1982, ABC did a story on 20/20 about anesthesia-related deaths. I was operated on in 1952 using ether, a common anesthetic at the time. Ether was very combustible and sometimes errors in the Operating Room caused explosions. Breathing tubes were sometimes accidently inserted into the stomach rather than the lungs, with disastrous consequence. Anesthesiologists had tanks of different gasses, oxygen, for example. When the patient needed some oxygen, sometimes a tank of something else was attached and death or brain damage ensued.

Anesthesiologists saw malpractice premiums jump from under $20,000 to over $50,000 a year. Anesthesiologists were "terrified," according to the president of the American Society of Anesthesiologists at the time. That Society formed a stand-alone organization solely devoted to patient safety. They read every malpractice suit against an anesthesiologist, figured out what went wrong and changed methods and procedures to make certain it did not happen again. Tanks of gasses were changed from a common fitting on the tank-top to unique ones that couldn't be inappropriately used. Monitoring devices were used to be certain that breathing tubes were correctly inserted. Most important, the death rate for anesthesiology is down to one in 200,000 – 300,000 patients. As a result, the cost of anesthesiologist's malpractice insurance has gone from one of the highest to one of the lowest.

Pharmacists and generic drug makers must do the same. They should push for drug naming and labeling standards. They must push for drug containers that provide the visually impaired with tactile help.

Change will not come quickly. In the meantime, you will have to be the one checking the prescription. If you see anything you do not think is correct, question your doctor or pharmacist.

Friends

An Iowan came home from work one day to find his wife in bed with his best friend. He took his gun and shot his wife and then called the police to surrender. When he was being questioned, he was asked why he hadn't shot the man as well. He answered, "Because he is my best friend."

Iowans understand the value of friendship, especially best friends. I remember asking my mother if she wanted to move to Florida if she ever retired. Her answer was no, all of her friends were nearby and she didn't want to leave them.

Youngsters, even those in Iowa, think they have many friends because they know so many of their classmates, or have so many Facebook "friends." But Facebook friends are not what we are talking about here. We are talking about friends who love you unconditionally, no matter what you have done or haven't done.

We are talking about a friend who will try his best to defend you from physical attack. Of course, the friend I am speaking of asks little in return–not even some variety in his daily food.

Okay, I am talking about a dog. Someone told President Clinton that if he wanted a friend in Washington D.C., he should get a dog. He did and he named him "Buddy." I followed suit and got my own dog, whom I called Buddy.

Much of the work I did on the Ohio Governor's Counsel on People with Disabilities exposed me to many guide dogs, known as working dogs. These dogs are highly trained and are devoted to serving their master, while calling little attention to themselves. In training, they are taught the skills their new master needs, be it guidance while walking or even retrieving dropped articles.

Service animals (they are mostly dogs, but this is not a requirement of law) can be taught many things. There are even dogs that help those with mental problems or are merely companion dogs.

Interestingly, service animals have many legal rights under the Americans with Disabilities Act (ADA). For example, a dog that is working can legally go anywhere the general public can go. This includes public transportation (planes, trains, and taxis) supermarkets, and other places where dogs are usually not allowed.

This even includes the hospital emergency rooms, although the staff will probably object. But the dog has the legal right to stay with his owner. The owner must be with the dog to enjoy these legal rights. Unfortunately, many people do not know the law and owners are often told that dogs are not allowed on an airplane and such. The dog wins almost invariably.

For those with PD who would like to have an elephant to lean on for walking, I would at least warn them about airline travel. Also it goes without saying that people expect your service animal to be house broken.

This and That

I should begin by disclosing to the new or infrequent reader, that I now write this column in North Carolina. There are two reasons for this: first is my retirement, and the second is to be further from angry vendors that I have offended in past columns. Many people cite the snow in Ohio as one of their reasons for moving further south. Not me. I enjoy seeing television accounts and video of snow in Ohio.

People here do have a southern way of dealing with life. For example I asked a medical specialist about what caused the difficulty I was experiencing. His answer was "Birthdays."

I liked that answer. He could have said that it was old age, but he didn't. He provided an answer to my question without telling me the usual 'You're just getting old." The lesson here is that your physician should always answer your questions truthfully, but kindly.

Another example of southern hospitality and charm was a fellow sitting behind me at a football game this past season. Whenever a player from either team would get injured and medics and assistant coaches had been dispatched to the injured athlete, he would give this advice to all within the sound of his voice (practically everyone), "Rub some dirt on it and walk it off."

Macho is football's middle name and usually the fellow will limp off the field in an attempt to not only feel macho, but also to protect his football scholarship. The big question for those with head trauma or high-level spinal cord injuries is, "Will this injury result in Parkinson's in later life?"

Some neurologists believe that trauma to the head, neck, or spine contributes to the damage in the substania nigra which is the area of the brain where such damage could eventually result in PD. It is thought by some that whiplash, concussion, and such, damages the blood-brain-barrier, allowing toxins to enter the brain. It may be decades before the PD makes itself known to its host.

Researchers are following head trauma cases to see if there is a direct link between head trauma and PD. There are many problems here because we cannot measure accurately the forces involved after the fact. We have no good idea about how fast PD progresses in a specific person.

Most researchers would advise people to err on the side of minimal trauma. Of course, boxing is all about causing trauma. Mohamed Ali absorbed many blows from his ring opponents and is now the most recognized person in the world with PD.

Turns out, I have a pony in this race. The reason we were attending the football game was to see our youngest child on the field.. She is a cheerleader at Wake Forest University. Cheerleading accounts for two-thirds of catastrophic injuries among girl athletes, not counting the possibility of PD later in life. Kaitlin has been injured when a partner accidently dropped her on her face and again when a pyramid collapsed with her atop.

The American Academy of Pediatrics recently called for cheerleading to be recognized as an official sport so it would have to follow the same rules for safety and coaching as gymnastics, soccer, basketball, and other popular girls' sports. I doubt that any cheerleader would go as far as wearing helmets and padding.

Next year she will be a senior and all of this will be behind her. She plans to go on for a degree in dentistry and inflict pain on others. (Below she stands atop a pyramid.)

Iowa Justice

When my mother was in her early 80s, she had her first automobile accident. She was leaving the supermarket and pulled out in front of an oncoming pickup truck she never saw. She was only shaken up, as were the couple in the pickup, but her car was totaled. The police issued her a ticket and a summons to appear in court.

On the appointed day, my mother, in her Sunday-best clothes, made her appearance in municipal court. The first case heard was a man accused of an aggravated assault. The accused was the scariest man my mother had ever seen. He pleaded "not guilty" and his case was scheduled for trial. Next was a man accused of armed robbery who also pleaded "not guilty" and was given a trial date. Third was a juvenile who, obviously had been here before, professed his innocence of car theft this time.

Mom's case was next. The bailiff read the charge of failure to yield right-of-way at an intersection. He concluded with, "How do you plead Mrs. Beetner?"

Mom was the first defendant to appear that morning without the benefit of legal council. It never occurred to her to engage a lawyer, given her obvious guilt.

While this was her first court appearance of her life, she was not unfamiliar with the workings of a court thanks to Judge Wapner. She responded "Guilty, your honor."

The judge looked up from the paperwork in front of him and fixed my mother in his stare.

"At last, a confessed criminal," he began. "$30,000 and five years. Next case."

Everyone in the court room stopped breathing and my mother's knees buckled slightly. Only when the bailiff began to laugh, did everyone realize the judge was having a bit of fun. The judge then changed his verdict to $25 and court costs.

What does this have to do with Parkinson's? Nothing really. If this disappoints you then you are focusing on your disease too much. Get out and have some fun.

I would like to thank all of those who provided inspiration and encouragement for my writing. I especially want to thank my editors (Lori Lovely, Sandy Beetner, Riley Beetner, and Kaitie Beetner.) They hid my poor spelling and my gross misuse of the language.

They are, however, not responsible for any errors. Some errors were due to my use of the mouse, hence providing the title of this book. Any other errors are my fault.

Made in the USA
Lexington, KY
13 June 2013